MOVING FROM FAILURE TO FULFILLMENT

STUCK

TONY GILMORE

UNSTUCK
Moving from Failure to Fulfillment

Tony Gilmore
ptgilla03@gmail.com

ISBN 978-1-943343-30-0
Printed in the USA.

Printed in the United States of America
www.destinedtopublish.com

Dedication

To my beautiful wife Angie and our exceptional children Sharon, Jordan, Tez, Amber, Daniel, and Gabbi, you are my inspiration. Without your love and support, this book would not have been possible.

STUCK

Contents

Introduction

There I was, sitting in a one-bedroom apartment in a horrible neighborhood and looking out the window as my car was being repossessed. Just a few months before, I'd had a good life, not easy but good. Now I sat there, divorced, bankrupt, and lost. How did I get there? I had no one to blame but myself. I looked around for others to blame. I wanted to blame my parents, my background, my neighborhood, just about anybody that I could think of blaming. But it was all my fault. My bad choices had brought me there. Now my car had been repossessed, all of my money was gone, my home was broken, and my life had fallen apart. I had never been that destitute before. I remember that, on nights when I couldn't sleep, I would take cold medicine just to get drowsy enough to go to sleep. My life was a train wreck, and it was all my fault. I'd been a Christian for about 9 years at that time.

And during that time, I'd experienced the peaks and valleys of faith. However, this season was different. I was not recovering. At that point in my life, I'd walked away from the faith a couple of years previously. The life that I wanted to live for God had become too difficult; I'd made it too hard. Notice I said I had made it too hard. I'd walked away from everything that was near and dear to me and headed into full blown sin. If you had run across me at that time, you wouldn't even have believed that I'd ever been a Christian. I tried over and over again but was not ready to let go of my sinful lifestyle. I lived in constant fear that, if it was my last day on earth, I would not go to heaven. And yet I didn't have the strength to stop. There were times when I felt like committing suicide just so that I would be done with all the suffering. I was mad at myself, mad at God, and mad at the world. I was totally and utterly lost.

As I sat in my one-bedroom apartment on that day, just a few days from being evicted because I could no longer afford my rent, deep thoughts of guilt and condemnation swam in my head. I knew I desperately needed God. However, I couldn't get past the fact that I had disgraced him by walking away. I couldn't get past the fact that my choices over the previous couple of years had separated me from God and, therefore, I felt I was no longer qualified to be his son.

At that moment, I felt like the only thing left was to end it all. Thoughts of suicide continued to run through my mind. I felt hopeless, helpless, and unable to reach out to God for help because I believed he no longer wanted me. I mean, what kind of God would give you everything then watch you turn your back on him and forgive you for it? I knew that, if I were God, I would not forgive me. However, in a moment of desperation, I cried out to him anyway. The story of the prodigal son flashed through my mind, and then I remembered how excited the father had been to welcome his son back. I cried out to God in that moment and said, "Father, I'm so sorry for what I've done over these past years. I'm so sorry for walking away from everything that you blessed me with and embarrassing you with my lifestyle. Father, please forgive me. I give up. I surrender. You can have my life. I've shown you what I can do with this life, and now I turn it over to you."

With tears in my eyes, I remember crying and asking God to forgive me but feeling deep down inside that he would not. At that moment, there was a knock at my door. It was my landlady. She said, "I don't know why, but I felt like I needed to come to your apartment to see how we could help you stay in it." She began to ask me what was going on in my life and why I couldn't pay my rent. I began to open my heart to her and share what was going on in my life. Then, with compassion in her eyes, she said, "We want to work with you. We want to help you stay in this apartment." That may not seem like much to you, but to me at the time, it was God saying, "I forgive you." I experienced the grace of God like I'd never experienced it before. I thought God could never forgive me after all that I'd done and after all the mistakes that I'd made, yet I sensed deep within my soul that God was restoring me. This would begin a process over the next year of God restoring my life and healing my shame.

I have written this book for everyone who's ever blown it and thought that God would never give them another chance. I have written it for everyone who is stuck in cycles of guilt, condemnation, and shame and is ready to be set free. When I look back, I'm reminded that I was no one special and that God did me no special favors. What I experienced is available to everyone who's willing to turn around and give their lives wholeheartedly to God.

The quote "Success is failure turned inside out," is inspiring but is often not lived out. In our culture, the fear of failure is so strong that many people don't even want to try. Many of the world's greatest inventors, artists, or innovators failed thousands of times before they came across their first success. Yet many of us consider our failures to carry negative connotations and stigma. I've learned over the years that failure is my friend, that when I embrace it, I'm actually setting myself up for success. This is one of the harder truths to understand in life: that failure isn't final. That on the other side of our biggest mistakes, we can enjoy our greatest successes if we learn.

Many people wallow in guilt and self-condemnation because their choices have led to things going wrong in their lives. Feelings of inferiority and inadequacy have caused many to simply be satisfied with whatever life has given them. They desire happiness and success but feel like they aren't worthy because of the lives that they've lived. They settle for mediocre, less-than-fulfilling lives because they no longer see themselves as deserving great ones. However, they are wrong.

God has a plan in store for you that is so great that it is beyond your wildest dreams. The only thing it requires is for you to get back up again. One of my favorite quotes follows: "Life has knocked me down a few times and shown me things I never wanted to see. I experience sadness and failures. But one thing for sure, I always get up." It's not how many times life knocks you down that determines the quality of your life: It's how many times you choose to get back up. Today we're going to get back up. We're going to dust ourselves off, pick up those dreams again, pick up those desires again, and live. We are not going to allow our mistakes or bad decisions to define us. Today, we're going to get back up.

In this book, I will give you the keys not only to getting back up again but also to finding a restored purpose and renewed sense of life. The steps that I'll give you are not theories, but there are proven methods to help you survive what you went through and thrive in spite of it. I believe these practical steps will help you regain your footing and live the life that you're supposed to live.

In the coming pages, I want to challenge you to emerge from the box of low self-esteem and low-level thinking and take your place as a king's child. Embark on a journey that will allow you to leave behind the negative thoughts and experiences that have kept you bound all of these years. My greatest desire is that, in reading this book, you will find the freedom that God says we can all have because of Jesus Christ. It is time. It is time to leave the past behind us and learn the lessons we were supposed to learn. Join me in this journey as we move from failure to fulfillment.

STUCK

Chapter 1

Failure Isn't Final

I've missed more than 9,000 shots in my career. I've lost almost 300 games. 26 times, I've been trusted to take the game winning shot and missed. I've failed over and over and over again in my life. And that is why I succeed. – Michael Jordan

> *Philippians 3:12-14 (TPT)*
>
> [12] *I admit that I haven't yet acquired the absolute fullness that I'm pursuing, but I run with passion into his abundance so that I may reach the purpose that Jesus Christ has called me to fulfill and wants me to discover.* [13] *I don't depend on my own strength to accomplish this;*[a] *however, I do have one compelling focus: I forget all of the past as I fasten my heart to the future instead.* [14] *I run straight for the divine invitation of reaching the heavenly goal and gaining the victory-prize through the anointing of Jesus.*

The way you perceive failure will determine your success. I love the above quote by Michael Jordan. He talks about all of the missed shots and all of the missed game winners that he has experienced yet they are the reasons for his success. Michael's view of failure made him an incredible success. Many of us take failure personally. We make failure part of who we are rather than part of what we've done. We say things like "I'm a failure," or believe that, because of one failure, we will never amount to anything. Sadly, many of us never get up from failed decisions, failed business deals, or failed relationships. We settle into lives that are less than what we want because we're afraid of failing again. However, that is not what God has called us to. God knew that we would all fail in some shape, form, or fashion, and that's why he sent Jesus. Jesus didn't come for perfect people. He came for people who would fail, and he is the hope that, when we fail, we can get back up again.

Throughout the Bible and throughout humanity, people have failed over and over again yet achieved success through their failures. Thomas Edison made a great statement: *I've not failed. I've just found* 10,000 *ways that won't work.* That's the right attitude when it comes to failure: that you are not a failure and you have not failed; you've just found several ways in which what you want to do won't work. But, when you get up again from failure and allow it to be the fuel that launches you into the future, you will be ready to go after the things that you can really achieve. It is a proper perspective of our past failures that allow us to be launched into future success. I love the way the Apostle Paul puts it in Philippians. He says,

> [12] *I admit that I haven't yet acquired the absolute fullness that I'm pursuing, but I run with*

> *passion into his abundance so that I may reach the purpose that Jesus Christ has called me to fulfill and wants me to discover.* [13] *I don't depend on my own strength to accomplish this;*[a] *however I do have one compelling focus: I forget all of the past as I fasten my heart to the future instead.* [14] *I run straight for the divine invitation of reaching the heavenly goal and gaining the victory-prize through the anointing of Jesus. (Philippians 3:12-14 (TPT))*

He gives us permission to let go of our past failures and move forward for future success. The ability to move beyond your past and into the future allows you to learn from your mistakes. You can't learn from your mistakes if you think you're a mistake.

Failure Precedes Success

One of the most powerful quotes I've ever come across is this one by Morihei Ueshiba: "Failure is the key to success; each mistake teaches us something." I listen to this, and it empowers me to take my failures and make them productive. Each time I experience failure, three thoughts help me to convert it into future success. The first one is "Don't take it personal." One of the missteps I previously used to take involved personalizing every mistake I made and saying that I was a mistake. I constantly lived in this place of defeat because I couldn't get past the fact that I thought the mistake was me. When I begin to learn that my failures weren't personal, meaning that I was not the failure, it was my idea that collapsed. This allowed me to separate myself from the failed attempt, relationship, idea, or anything that I was trying to accomplish. Through this thought process, I gained the greatest value and learned the greatest lessons from the mistakes that I would make. The lesson: Don't take failure personally.

The second thought that helped me process my failures and turn them into successes was this: "Don't have a pity party." Pity parties don't help anybody. They're simply opportunities to self-loathe, to speak self-defeating thoughts, to keep you wounded in the cycle of failure. I love this quote from Joyce Meyer: "You can be pitiful or powerful, but you can't be both." What an empowering statement! You can choose to be pitiful, or you can choose to be powerful, but you can't be both. So I chose to be powerful. That meant that, instead of beating myself up over mistakes that I made, I would continue to build myself up. One way may not have worked but there was another that would work. Like Edison, I just found 10,000 ways that wouldn't work. When I adopted this mindset, I was able to continue to press toward the answer and the success that I was looking for. The lesson: Don't have a pity party.

The last thought was "Don't miss the lesson." Taking a failure personally and then launching into a full-blown pity party took away my ability to learn what I was supposed to learn from it. As I stated early in the chapter, failure is the key to success; each mistake teaches us something. When we take our mistakes personally and walk into pity parties, our minds lose the ability to really learn from what we missed so that we can gain the greatest value from our mistakes or failures. We have to go back and analyze where we went wrong without identifying with the

wrong. Honestly, why waste a good failure? You failed anyway. Whether it was a relationship, a business idea, or your wanting to experience a life change, the failure is already there. Why not get something out of it? The lesson: Don't miss the lesson.

Rising Above Failure

I was sitting in the chair of a therapist, feeling defeated, demoralized, and hopeless. She began helping me rehearse the years of failed relationships and failed opportunities in my life. As I laid out the gory details of my failed marriage and how I'd failed as a husband and a person, my therapist took me through a series of questions. These questions began to uncover some of the paradigms that I'd developed in my mind regarding relationships. I fully expected her to spend most of our time dissecting why my marriage had failed, but she spent it digging into the time before I was married. It didn't make sense to me at all. I mean, I was there because my marriage had failed and I was a failure, and so I needed help navigating my failure. But she took me to a place in my childhood that I really didn't want to face, a painful place that I'd blocked out for years and that she said was affecting how I handled my relationships.

Because of all of the relationships that had failed in my life, I knew that the people I was in the relationships with weren't necessarily to blame. I pointed the finger squarely at myself. I knew that there was something wrong with me and that was why they weren't working. However, I didn't know how far back my thoughts went. It turned out that my thoughts of failed relationships started with my first relationship with a member of the opposite sex: my relationship with my mother. My mother lived with mental illness, and, as I grew up, it would cause me to develop a mindset regarding women that was both unhealthy and dishonorable.

The therapist began to take me through a series of events I experienced as a young man that caused me to think that my mom's illness was my fault. This thought that I had failed my mother as a son would rear its ugly head in every relationship that I had going forward. I thought that, when a person really got to know me, I would fail them just like I'd failed my mother. I thought that, if I'd been a better son, my mother's illness would have taken a different shape. Therefore, I considered her illness to be a manifestation of my failure as a son. What I didn't know was that this sense of being a failure would cause me to walk into every relationship after that thinking that I would fail in it too.

In our sessions, my therapist allowed me to identify the root cause of many of the failures that I had experienced in relationships and in life. I had adopted the mindset that I was a failure, and it had become a self-fulfilling prophecy. Through the word of God and the efforts of this amazing counselor, I begin to dig myself out of the failures of my past and into the promise of my future. I was able to understand that I did not fail as a son, and dealing with that failure would allow me to unravel the thoughts that made me feel that I was a failure in everything else. The reality was that I had failed in some situations, but I wasn't a failure. At that point, I was able to look back on my life and learn the lesson I needed to learn to succeed in life, in love, and in purpose. Today, I am in an amazing relationship with my wife of 16 years, and I have been blessed with a beautiful family. I have a great career and an awesome life, and it's all because I realized failure wasn't final. Failure is simply the platform God would use to bring me into ultimate success.

Things to Remember

- *A proper perspective of our failures allows us to launch ourselves into future success.*
- *You can't learn from your mistakes if you think you're a mistake.*

Slow and Steady

Lamentations 3:25-26 (ESV)

[25] *The Lord is good to those who wait for him, to the soul who seeks him.* [26] *It is good that one should wait quietly for the salvation of the Lord.*

Slow and steady wins the race. – Robert Lloyd

The Crockpot and the Microwave

My wife makes an incredible pot roast. I mean, when she's done, the meat falls off the bone, and it is just succulent. As I watch the process that she follows to make the pot roast, I often want to rush it. Picture this: She places the meat in a crockpot and allows it to cook for 12 hours. The smells waft through the house. My anticipation is high, and I am ready to eat as soon as she starts cooking it. Waiting 12 hours for this thing to cook is almost like torture. I'm ready to eat after one or two hours, but she says we have to wait 12 hours for it to cook. I'm anxious, I'm hungry, and, most of all, I can't wait to get the finished product.

I didn't understand why this process took so long until I interrupted it to get a taste of the meat one day. I grabbed a piece of meat after it had cooked for only a few hours. To my surprise and disappointment, it was still red on the inside. It didn't have the same texture as her typical roast, and I could almost feel myself getting sick because I was sure uncooked meat couldn't be good for me. I learned a valuable lesson on that day. The roast preparation process had to be allowed to continue to the end, or the roast would not be suitable for consumption. It's the same thing with us. We must be patient as God takes us through the process of restoration. I'm sure that, like me, you would like for this process to move very quickly. When we decide to turn back to God, we immediately want our reputations restored, our credibility back, and any loss to be instantaneously regained. However, it doesn't work like that. Trust is gained slowly but can be lost in a moment. That's why we must have patience and be consistent in our behavior to regain what we lost with our bad choices. We must understand that there will be a season where we put in maximum effort but get little response. It will be important then to recognize the season that we're in : a season of sowing.

Identifying the Season

I believe one of the keys to navigating the process of restoration that God takes us through is understanding the seasons. We understand the concept that winter, spring, summer, and fall exist. We understand this so well that we don't get frustrated in the winter because we know spring is going to come. We understand it so well that, even in the heat of the summer, we endure it because we know that the cooler fall is coming. Well that's how it works with our lives. When we understand that the current season is temporary and that it will end and lead to a better season, we can better withstand its challenges. That's how we understand God's process of restoration. Understanding that God loves us, believes in us, and has a plan for our lives allows us to withstand the season that we're in no matter how uncomfortable it is because we know a better time is coming.

The process that God takes us through has valleys and mountaintops. It has high moments, and it has low moments. And once we comprehend that everything God allows in our lives is for our good, we gain the ability to step back and identify the season that we're in. The challenge is that, sometimes, the pain of the present is so extreme that we don't take a moment to identify the season. And, sometimes, the discomfort of the season is so great that we don't have the ability to analyze what's going on. However, when we truly see that God loves us, has a great plan for us, and is working all things out for our good, we will be able to navigate each season and get what we're supposed to out of it. In one of the Scriptures that has helped me tremendously, Jesus talks about the parable of corn. He gives us insight into how God's process works for us:

> [28] *The earth produces by itself, first the blade, then the ear, then the full grain in the ear.* [29] *But when the grain is ripe, at once he puts in the sickle, because the harvest has come.* (Mark 4:28-29 (ESV))

In this parable, we can see and identify a principle of God's process. The first thing we identify is that He says the earth produces the blade first by itself. One of the things that I noticed about corn or anything that grew from the ground was that the growth process didn't start above the ground. It actually started with the roots developing beneath the surface. So, when you understand this, you comprehend that, in the seasons of God's process for your life, there are times when you're hidden and your best efforts aren't noticed. When you don't get any accolades. No one celebrates you. No one pats you on the back. In these seasons, I believe God is building the foundation for what you will be later on. During the process of your restoration, for a season, no one really believes that you've changed. In that period, God develops in you the type of behavior that exists even when no one is looking.

This is the unseen season. He develops you behind the scenes. He hides you from the crowd. This season of hiding can be so frustrating for those of us who want to earn the trust of those we hurt, who want more and know that God has more in store for us. But the season is necessary because, without it, we will not fully develop into the people whom God has called us to be. The hiding is not meant to hurt us but to help us understand that, what we do, we do for an audience of one. We're not looking for accolades, great names, or fame and stardom. We're simply looking to fulfill our purpose to the glory of God. Also, in this season of hiding, we actually get to make mistakes without being in full view of everyone. This season is meant to bless us, not to hurt us.

Second, the blade. Now you get to see flashes of what God has called you to be. God begins to open doors for you to get a glimpse of the purpose that He has for your life. In the first season, God is refining and developing you. In the second phase, He's allowing your character to develop so that you can begin to build confidence and He can sharpen you for what He's called you to. The dangerous thing about the blade season is that, when you begin to see fruit and people begin to notice you, there is a temptation to believe that you've arrived. Many people stop at this point because they grow satisfied with just being able to survive. They're simply happy that someone has noticed the changes in their lives. However, this is just the blade. It's really just the beginning, and if you lose the hunger for God and for growth, you could get stuck here.

Third is the ear. You have allowed some roots to dig in where your character is concerned, you've allowed some growth to take place, and you hunger for more of what God has for you. The ear is probably one of the most painful parts of the process. In this season, you've tasted the fruit of the life God has for you, but God has started to put his finger on another area of your life. You feel that you've achieved so much and even begin to think that you are better than others, only to find out that God is not through with you yet. In this third phase, God begins to move and deal with some of the deeper challenges of your life.

In the first two phases, things seem to be moving at a steady pace; you seem to be growing and developing at a steady pace. But in the third phase, with the ear coming, things begin to slow down. This is where frustration can begin to seep in because you have allowed God to develop your character but a new defect has been revealed to you. When the corn is underground, you can't really see what it's going to be unless you know the seed that was planted. Every seed has roots, and all seeds have some blade or stock or something. But it's when the fruit or the ear appears that you know what is really meant to be.

In this third phase, you come into an awareness of who you are and begin reflecting more of a Christlike character. This is the place where you begin to see your uniqueness and your true self come into play. It's your journey; it's what you've walked through; it's what you've overcome; it's who you have been formed into. This third leg of the journey, when the true essence of what the seed is supposed to be becomes evident, is the difficult side of the developmental process. Many people don't make it to this point. I'm reminded of the Scripture that says many are called but few are chosen. This season, this part of God's process may be too painful for many people to endure. Why is it so difficult? Because this part of the process means that you have to look back at some of the most painful parts of your life and allow God to heal you. This third leg requires us to look back at our childhood pain, our adult mistakes, and the things that we've allowed to identify us and to challenge those things.

When you allow God to take you through this season or phase, you are ready for Him to move you to the next level. If you don't identify the season for what it is, you could get stuck in it, in bitterness, and in unforgiveness towards others and yourself. It can feel like God is punishing you because of the season that He's allowing you to go through, bringing back all of this stuff so that you can deal with it. However, once you know that this is a part of your process and you can identify the season, you can allow your pain to become your platform. At this point, your purpose is ready to be fulfilled. When you allow God to do His perfect work in this season, you become ready for the harvest. You are now ready for God to move you into the purpose and plan that He created you for all along.

God's process in your life must be allowed to be completed, or you will not be fully prepared for His call. When you are underdeveloped, you have the potential to hurt people just like the meat had the potential to make me sick. God's prepares his called in a crockpot, not a microwave. He has to allow the seasoning of time, tests, and trials to take place to prepare them properly. James puts it like this:

> 2 *My brothers and sisters, be very happy when you are tested in different ways.* 3 *You know that such testing of your faith produces endurance.* 4 *Endure until your testing is over. Then you will be mature and complete, and you won't need anything.* (James 1:2-4 (GW))

As God takes you through your process, He develops something inside of you. We live in a culture of quick fixes and meteoric rises. Many often see their destiny as a place to get to rather than focusing on the journey experience. Our world offers stories of people who have been thrust into stardom, only to become epic failures because they didn't have the right foundation to build on. Even in the church, men and women of God are placed in high positions due to their gifts or talents, but they don't have a solid ethical base to build on. Decades of moral failures, unethical practices, and shady dealings cause some Christians' lives to look more like scenes out of *The Young and the Restless* than the Kingdom of God. People who are called by God, anointed to do great works for the Kingdom of God, sometimes end up crashing and burning under the pressure of increased notoriety and fame because they didn't allow God to finish His process.

I'm Ready

I was the Athletic Director at a local church. I knew that God was calling me to pastor a church at some point, and I started to get antsy. I had spent several weeks working on a discipleship plan and was starting to really feel the desire to be a Senior Pastor. I turned in the 20-page document to my leader, who said he would read it and get back to me. I was so excited. I knew he would take one look at my plan, know it was from God, and start my program the following week. A few days went by, and I got increasingly frustrated that I hadn't gotten an answer. I begin thinking, "What is going on with him? Why hasn't he gotten back to me? What is he waiting on?" A week later he called me into his office. I was beyond excited and ready to move forward. This was my big break. I started thinking, "He is going to want to start a new church and put me in charge of it. He is going to send me with 300 people to launch a brand-new campus. I can't wait to tell my wife Angie and our kids. This is going to be amazing."

He picked up my document and handed it to me with a guarded look on his face. He said, "Tony, I'm sorry but we can't use your plan." Immediately, my face dropped, and my blood started to boil. It was like something out of a movie. I imagined jumping across the desk and making him eat my document (Hey, I'm a work in progress). I looked at him and asked why, but all he said was "Not right now." I knew he'd never read the plan.

I was infuriated! I couldn't believe he'd said no. Then I thought, "I'm not doing anything else for this ministry. I'm done." I went home and started to pray—well, started to vent to God. Not much prayer was going on. Then it hit me: "I'm going to start my own church." This situation was God telling me it was time to go. I set up a meeting with my pastor and told him the news: "Pastor, God has called me to start a church."

He looked at me as if I had just cussed in his office. He said, "Let's give this a week and get back together." During that week, I prayed/vented more and more. I knew God was telling me it was time. I had the church name and the vision statement, and, in my head, I was building my team. I was ready to go.

A week went by, and I walked into the office to meet my pastor. To my surprise, he had another gentleman in the room, another pastor I knew very well. As we began our conversation, the other pastor asked, "What's in your heart to do?"

I quickly said, "To launch a life-giving church." I knew that no one could argue with that.

Then he said something that blew my mind. He and my pastor looked at each other, then my pastor wrote a phrase on a piece of paper. He lifted the paper so that I could see it. It said, "Senior Pastor."

I began to shout on the inside. "Yes, they see it. They get it. Now is the time." My heart started racing; it was about to happen.

Then the other pastor said something that left me speechless. He said, "We believe you are called to be a senior leader, but we want you to wait a year."

A thought ran through my mind: *What?! A year?! They must be crazy. I'm not waiting a year. Nope. Nope. Nope. Now they are going to make me launch tomorrow. Now I'm really done.*

I went home and prayed for real this time; I did not vent. It was there that the Holy Spirit said, "I have not changed your assignment. You are to remain here."

I was upset, frustrated, and confused. I made a decision: *I'm going to stay, but I'm not going to give my best. I'm just going to bide my time until God releases me.* But the Holy Spirit would not let me just coast. In such moments, God is testing us to see whether we were ready to handle our own. If I couldn't continue to give my all to someone else's when God had told me to, what would I do when I had my own. God wouldn't let me do what I wanted to do? It was a test.

After I got over my feelings, I went back to both pastors and told them I would wait. What I didn't know was that something was awaiting me on the other side of obedience.

A few months later, I got a phone call from a young lady who was going to be coming to our church. She had heard about our sports program and wanted to help. That lady turned out to be the wife of the coach of the St. Louis Rams. She and her husband, the new coach of the Rams, were moving to our city and would be making our church their home. They would become two of my staunchest supporters and would contribute greatly to the program, allowing us to grow from 300 students to over 1,000 students. If I had done my own thing, I would have missed one of the greatest blessings and lessons I ever received. Through this experience, I learned the value of allowing God to finish his process. I was ready to go, but God wasn't ready for me to go. He was deepening my character and creating a firmer foundation by making me wait longer than I wanted. God's process can sometimes be slow, but it's certain.

Things to Remember

- *God's process of restoration is slow but certain.*
- *God prepares his called in a crockpot, not a microwave.*

Chapter 3

Flawed but Faithful

I love the story of Superman because it has so many similarities to real life. I know you may consider this to be a stretch, but if you think about the story, you'll realize it has parallels to life all over it. When I was growing up, Superman was my hero because I saw him as having no weakness, no flaws. He was the perfect superhero because he seemed invincible: There were no chinks in his armor. He was stronger than everyone, faster than everyone, and could see through walls. Who wouldn't want to be like that?

Imagine my disappointment when kryptonite was introduced into the series. I couldn't believe that Superman actually had a weakness after all those years of seeing him as the perfect person: no weaknesses, no flaws, simple perfection. Yet he had this one weakness that he couldn't overcome. No matter how strong or fast he was, when kryptonite came on the scene, he became a mortal. However, like in most movies, the hero found a way to overcome his weakness and still save the world. That's my true definition of a hero. A hero isn't someone who never experiences adversity, never walks through struggles, or never has to deal with challenges. Right in the face of weakness, disappointments, and challenges, the hero always finds a way to overcome them and do what needs to be done. What I loved about Superman was that he never allowed kryptonite to keep him down; he never allowed it to define him. He simply stayed faithful to the cause and found a way right in the midst of his weakness to overcome it and do what needed to be done.

We Are All Flawed

One of the greatest tricks that the enemy plays on us is convincing us to disqualify ourselves from God's will if we have flaws. He tells us over and over again that, because of our weaknesses, because of the things that aren't right with us, God can't use us. I have a secret for you: We are all flawed. Every single one of us, no matter how gifted, talented, or anointed, is flawed. What does it mean to be flawed? It means we're blemished, damaged, and imperfect in some way, that we have a weakness of character operating in our lives. Often, we think of the heroes of the Bible and we imagine God used them because they were perfect and had it all together. However, that is not the truth. Some of the greatest men and women in the Bible were greatly flawed, yet God used them greatly. Take a look at this list:

- *Moses was a murderer;*
- *Jacob was a liar;*
- *Gideon was fearful;*

- *Elijah battled depression;*
- *Peter was prideful.*

Many of us could never believe the moments of weakness that these heroes experienced. We've always thought of the Bible heroes' as people of great faith with strong moral compasses. Yet they were flawed just like us. The Apostle Paul gives us a picture of what God looks for when he chooses a man or a woman to fulfill his will on earth:

> [26] *Notice among yourselves, dear brothers, that few of you who follow Christ have big names or power or wealth.* [27] *Instead, God has deliberately chosen to use ideas the world considers foolish and of little worth in order to shame those people considered by the world as wise and great.* [28] *He has chosen a plan despised by the world, counted as nothing at all, and used it to bring down to nothing those the world considers great,* [29] *so that no one anywhere can ever brag in the presence of God.* (1 Corinthians 1:26–29 (TLB))

The Scripture gives us insight into the mind of God. He is not looking for the superspiritual, the supermoral, or the superelite in our society. However, he is looking for a quality of character that is beyond perfection and flawless living. The character that he's looking for in every person that he uses is faithfulness. So, no matter how flawed we are or how glaring our weaknesses, if we remain faithful to God's call, he can use us in ways that we would never imagine. To be faithful means to have a constant unwavering commitment and duty. It means that, no matter what happens, how many times it happens, or how many times I messed up, I'm going to keep showing up and moving forward. It simply means I won't quit. My faithfulness has the ability to overcome my flaws. When I stay committed to God's purpose, I eventually overcome every flaw that once held me down.

What I love about the men and women who have done incredible things in this world is that they didn't allow their weaknesses to stop them from moving forward. They had such unwavering belief in what they had to contribute to society that they kept going in spite of themselves. When a man or woman has that kind of faithfulness to God, nothing is impossible to them. No matter how many times they fail, they keep going because they know they have to. Faithful people realize that they're going to make mistakes but God's grace is enough to help them get back up again. They realize they're not always going to win, but they won't stop trying. They realize that nothing is impossible to them that believe.

God is looking for this faithfulness of character in the people that he uses, not perfection. John Maxwell puts it thus: "When you continue serving with faithfulness, humility, and right motives, you're making room in your life for God to fulfill his purposes in you when the time is right." When someone continues to serve faithfully, they're positioning themselves to see the fullness of God's purpose come to pass in their lives because they didn't quit. That is what faithfulness does; it gives us the ability to keep fighting, keep moving, and keep believing even when we feel like quitting.

Oftentimes, we want to be faithful, but we don't really understand what faithfulness looks like. Many of us have never seen faithfulness modeled. A lot of what we've seen entails people giving up or quitting. Faithfulness is the ability to finish what you started and not to give up on what you believe in, even if your weaknesses and flaws sometimes cause you to get in your own way. I believe that there is a path to faithfulness and once we learn how to walk in it, we can get back up and keep moving no matter how many times we fail or make a misstep. The question is how do we get up when we fail? I've learned to get up in three ways every time I've failed:

1. *The first thing you must do is forgive yourself. We often think that forgiving others alone is a pathway to freedom, to leaving the bitterness of the past behind us. But we often don't realize that the hardest person to forgive is oneself. Lack of forgiveness for ourselves will keep us stuck in cycles of failure, and that will not allow us to learn from our mistakes.*

2. *Next, we must focus on putting the past behind us. This doesn't mean that we should forget the past, but it does mean that we should only look back with purpose in mind. The days of guilt and condemnation are over. The time of beating ourselves up over our mistakes is done. We should simply look back to learn, grow, and get better. Putting our past behind us does not mean never thinking of it again. It simply means thinking of it differently when we do look back. This ability to look back without beating ourselves up will allow us to gain the most value out of understanding the things we got wrong.*

3. *Lastly, we must forge ahead. That means that, although we made mistakes and did some things wrong, we must apologize and make amends for our wrongs. But we should not stay there. Once we've done those things and taken responsibility for the people we've hurt, it'll be time to forge ahead and do the things we were created to do. You can't look backward and forward at the same time. Don't cheat on your future success by spending all your time thinking about your past mistakes. You are only cheating yourself out of being the person you were created to be. Your flaws, your failings, and your mistakes are all part of the person that God is making you into. Not one moment is wasted; your time would only be wasted if you didn't allow it to make you better.*

Grace for Weaknesses

I'm reminded of a dramatic encounter with the grace of God in my life years ago. I had gone through a divorce. I knew I was called to something greater in my life, but I couldn't get past the mistakes that I'd made. My marriage had ended, and I felt like a failure. Immaturity on both of our parts had resulted in our causing each other hurt and pain over the years. However, I was stuck with the sting that I could not make it work. I remember knowing that God had called me to something greater and sensing that there was more to my life than I could see but not being able to emerge from this failure. To me, there was nothing worse than knowing there was more but not feeling like I deserved it. I walked under a constant cloud of guilt and shame. It affected how I worked, lived, and parented. I simply believed that I didn't deserve blessings or God's best in my life because I was not perfect. Then God began to show me the incredible immenseness of his grace in my life. He began to tell me how I was forgiven and was his righteousness, not because of a perfect performance but because of my faith in Jesus. The Apostle Paul gives us insight into how God views our weaknesses:

> [9] *But He has said to me, "My grace is sufficient for you [My lovingkindness and My mercy are more than enough—always available—regardless of the situation]; for [My] power is being perfected [and is completed and shows itself most effectively] in [your] weakness." Therefore, I will all the more gladly boast in my weaknesses, so that the power of Christ [may completely enfold me and] may dwell in me.* [10] *So I am well pleased with weaknesses, with insults, with distresses, with persecutions, and with difficulties, for the sake of Christ; for when I am weak [in human strength], then I am strong [truly able, truly powerful, truly drawing from God's strength].* (1 Corinthians (12:9-10))

He began to show me Scripture after Scripture on how His grace was sufficient for my weakness. He said that, when I was weak, I was at my strongest because it was my weaknesses that kept me dependent on Him. He allowed me to come to the end of myself so that I could see that I couldn't do anything without Him. I thought I knew the grace of God when I worked everything out right. However, it was in my greatest failings, my most apparent flaws, and my biggest mistakes that His grace showed up the most for me. It was a supernatural revelation that, apart from Him, I could do nothing, but, in Him, I could do all things that allowed me to get up and move forward. He allowed me to see that it wasn't my perfect performance that qualified me to fulfill His will for my life, it was His grace that qualified me to have his best in my life. I saw for the first time through new lenses that, as long as I stayed faithful, he could work through my flaws and, as long as I kept getting up after falling down, he could work with my weaknesses. I learned without a doubt that I was flawed, but, as long as I was faithful, God could do anything through my life.

Things to Remember

- *We are all flawed, but God's grace covers us.*
- *Forgiving yourself is the key to freedom.*
- *God looks for our faithfulness in spite of our flaws.*

Chapter 4

Quitters Never Win

Character makes trust possible, and trust is the foundation of leadership. It's true that charisma can make a person stand out for a moment, but character sets a person apart for a lifetime. – *John Maxwell*

> Galatians 6:9 (ERV)
>
> 9 *We must not get tired of doing good. We will receive our harvest of eternal life at the right time. We must not give up.*

One of the key things that I've learned over the years is that your character will determine your legacy. I've seen so many people come through my doors with great talent and great charisma but no character. They came as a flash in the pan, a great addition in the moment, only to crash and burn just as quickly as they came in. Character is one of the key factors that will take us from failure to fulfillment. Character understands that it's the long game of consistent behavior that allows people to walk through the doors of total fulfillment. I often see people who want to get to where they're going so quickly that they're willing to cut corners and do whatever to make it happen. Then they get to where they think they want to be and do not have the character to sustain themselves.

What is character? Character encompasses the mental and moral qualities distinctive to an individual. It's described as a person's good reputation. I read a book a few years ago called *If You Were God, Would You Choose You?* It was a book by a guy named Rick Renner. In it, he lays out the qualities of people that God would look to promote and give great influence to. He talks about one of the greatest killers of purpose is quitting in one of the chapters. He says that many people start off well and go after their dreams, passion, and vision with all their might but quit at the first sign of trouble. They don't realize that, over the course of time, they develop reputations for being quitters.

People can overcome so many different things, so many different challenges. I simply believe that there is no challenge so great that someone cannot overcome it to do what God has given them to do. However, one thing can't be overcome: It is when someone quits. One of my good friends would say on a regular basis, "If you don't quit, you win." However, many of us quit before we reach our goals because things become difficult and hard to overcome. With this thought in mind, the Apostle Paul wrote this incredible portion of Scripture that has brought so many people encouragement over the years:

> [9]*We must not get tired of doing good. We will receive our harvest of eternal life at the right time. We must not give up.* (Galatians 6:9 (ERV))

Paul tells us not to be tired of doing good because we will reap a harvest. We should not give up. For many of us, quitting has become what we do. Paul encourages us, saying that, if we don't quit or give up, we will get our harvest at just the right time. I believe that the quality of character that keeps us from giving up when things get hard is called persistence. With persistence, we keep moving forward in spite of opposition, obstacles, and discouragement. That bulldog tenacity keeps us going when we feel like quitting, when the world has told us no, or when we're just tired from the grind. Persistence helps us not to quit when everything in us and around us tells us that what we're going after won't happen.

When the voices around you become loud, attacking the very thing that God said you could have or the dream that is deeply entrenched in who you are, persistence causes you to get up every morning. Even though no door is open, no job has called you back, and you haven't found Mrs. or Mr. Right, persistence helps you continue believing that what's in your heart will come to pass even when nothing around you says that it will. The Bible gives us this incredible picture of what it means to be persistent in the face of opposition. The story of blind Bartimaeus is inspiring and encouraging about how God views our persistence regarding what we want from him. In Mark 10:46-52, we read the following:

> [46] *And they came to Jericho. And as he was leaving*
> *Jericho with his disciples and a great crowd,*
> *Bartimaeus, a blind beggar, the son of Timaeus, was*
> *sitting by the roadside.* [47] *And when he heard that*

> *it was Jesus of Nazareth, he began to cry out and say, "Jesus, Son of David, have mercy on me!" [48] And many rebuked him, telling him to be silent. But he cried out all the more, "Son of David, have mercy on me!" [49] And Jesus stopped and said, "Call him." And they called the blind man, saying to him, "Take heart. Get up; he is calling you." [50] And throwing off his cloak, he sprang up and came to Jesus. [51] And Jesus said to him, "What do you want me to do for you?" And the blind man said to him, "Rabbi, let me recover my sight." [52] And Jesus said to him, "Go your way; your faith has made you well." And immediately he recovered his sight and followed him on the way. (Mark 10:46-52 (ESV))*

Bartimaeus believed so deeply that Jesus could heal him that he did not allow the voices of opposition to stop him from receiving what God had for him. He did not allow the crowd yelling at him or even the fact that Jesus did not turn around immediately to stop him from going after what he knew God had in store for him. He had heard the stories of Jesus and how he had healed people, and he wanted his sight back. If he had given up after the first time he had called out to Jesus, what would have happened? If he had given up after the people had begun to speak to him and to tell him to leave Jesus alone, what would have happened? I'll tell you what would have happened: He would still have been blind.

Because of his persistence, he walked away able to see. The key is, if you quit, you'll have what you already had. All the efforts, all the money, all the things that you put into making your dreams come to pass would be wasted, and you would have what you started out with: nothing. But, when you persist, you have the opportunity to have God perform a miracle on your behalf. When you persist, you open the door for God to open doors for you. When you persist, you have the opportunity to see God overcome all of your obstacles. I don't know what obstacles you have in front of you. I don't know what words you have been shouting at yourself. But I want you to know that, if you don't quit and you persist, you will reap the harvest.

The Day I Felt Like Quitting

A few years back, I started a program to enable inner city kids to play sports. I put so much work into this program. I made phone calls, went to schools to recruit, and talked to local sports teams, asking for their help. I recruited volunteers, and, anything you could think of doing, I put the work in. I was so confident that the first day of signups would yield hundreds of kids that I was excited. On that day, I took my son and my daughter, and we went to the front of the office at the local recreation center, ready to sign parents up. In the first hour, no one showed up. In the second hour, no one showed up. In the third hour, one parent showed up with her two kids. Those would be our only sign-ups for that entire day.

I was devastated! On that day, I remember thinking how I had missed God and that I'd made a mistake. I had never felt that low in my life. I now had to go back to all the people that I'd told that this was God and that it would be successful and tell them that I was a huge failure. I called my wife on that day to tell her what had happened and that I had probably missed God. She began to encourage me by telling me I hadn't missed God and that I needed to keep moving forward. I did not feel like moving forward. I was ready to quit. Well, because of her encouragement, I kept moving forward.

On that day, I made a choice not to quit. I would be persistent and find new ways to bring success to the moment. I went back to the drawing board, reached out to new people, found different ways to advertise, and started my first season with 75 kids. Although still disappointed, I decided to treat these 75 kids like I would have treated the 300 that I had been expecting. Little did I know that this group of 75 would eventually turn into over 1,000 kids. I had partnerships with the Saint Louis Cardinals, the Saint Louis Rams, and Saint Louis Public Schools. The concept that had started as just a thought in my mind would eventually become something bigger than I'd ever expected. I learned a valuable lesson in that season: the only way to lose was to quit. If I had quit, thousands of kids would have missed out on hearing the gospel.

From this program, kids got scholarships to go to college. Others went on to college and made their mark in other areas. When I look back at how badly I wanted to quit and how much persistence played a part in my sticking with it, I am reminded of the Apostle Paul's statement: that we are not to grow tired in doing good; if we don't quit, we will reap a harvest. Persistence gave me the strength not to quit when I felt like quitting.

Things to Remember

- *Your character will determine your legacy.*
- *Persistence is the key to finishing strong.*
- *Quitting is most tempting right before a breakthrough.*

Chapter 5

Patience: More Than a Virtue

Hebrews 6:12 (TLB)

> [12] *Then, knowing what lies ahead for you, you won't become bored with being a Christian nor become spiritually dull and indifferent, but you will be anxious to follow the example of those who receive all that God has promised them because of their strong faith and patience.*

Patience is bitter, but its fruit is sweet. – Aristotle

Your ability to be patient will determine how much you accomplish in life. In the last chapter, we talked about quitting. My question to you concerns how many times you quit because what you wanted was taking too long to come to pass. I believe that one of the major reasons why people quit is that they don't have the patience to wait for whatever takes a while. Most people don't understand that, if you're going to do something significant, it isn't going to happen overnight. I'm reminded of seeing some of my favorite actors and actresses when they have breakthrough roles in Hollywood. Often, we see them and are like "Wow! They were an overnight success. I never heard of them before they came out with this movie." However when I look at a show or sitcom from years ago, I'll see this actor, who I thought was just coming onto the scene as a child actor in a 1980s sitcom. In my view, they were an overnight success, but, if you were to ask them, they would say success came with years of hard work, belief, and patience.

Many of us start on our journeys with great enthusiasm, high energy, and great belief that what we're going after will come to pass. However, the greatest test of how much we believe in what we're doing is patience. Most of us don't understand that this journey of patience is actually one of God's greatest tools for developing us. In the season of waiting, God does some of his deepest work within our hearts. This place of waiting, I affectionately call "the in-between season." The in-between season is the time between the promise and fulfillment. I often think of it as being divided into these phases: the promise, the process, and then the procurement.

First, we receive the promise. It can be something more from God or a promise that we've made to ourselves to accomplish a certain goal. Every time we go after it, we're actually signing up for a process. This process is the place of development; it's a place of growth where our faith will be tested and our paradigm will be shifted. I have found this to be true: The worst you will ever be at any task is at the beginning. No matter how excited you are, no matter how gifted you may be when you launch something, that is the worst you'll ever be at it. That's actually a reason to rejoice because, no matter how bad you think your performance is, you know it can only get better.

Here, patience is needed the most. We have to be patient with ourselves, we have to be patient with the process, and, most of all, we have to be patient with God. James 1:4 says, "*And true patience brought on by endurance will equip you to complete the long journey and cross the finish line—mature, complete, and wanting nothing.*" James lets us know that patience is actually working on our behalf and developing us into what we need for the journey ahead of us. When we despise patience, we actually despise the process.

The In-Between

In August 1442, Christopher Columbus set out to find America. Part of the way through his journey, the needle on his compass no longer pointed to the North Star, which was helping guide them to their destination. Instead, the needle began pointing to the northwest and continued as the journey progressed. Columbus made no mention of this to his men, knowing that his crew members were prone to panic when they didn't know their destination. But, after several days, the pilots took notice and became anxious. That made the men worry.

The story says that the men became homesick and fearful and threatened to turn back from the trip to America. Yet, because of their perseverance, on October 12, 1492, they found America. But the story reminds me that there will be times in our journey when we feel lost because it's taken so long to come to pass. When we are in between the promise and provision, we can often feel lost and want to settle for less than we set out for. However, remember that this is all a part of the process. This is all a part of moving you out of your comfort zone and into your impact zone. As you continue to move further in this journey, you will have to lay down the desire for comfort so that you can embrace what God has for you. The in-between season is a difficult one to navigate, but you must go through it if you're going to move from failure to fulfillment.

The Three Temptations of In-Between

As you navigate the in-between season, you will face three temptations that will surely cause you to want to quit and hit what I call one of the off-ramps of destiny. The first one is your flesh. Your flesh will want to make it happen sooner than it should happen. This is where you will be tempted to rely on self-effort and to work to make God's promise come to pass. You will be tempted to look too far ahead and not give enough attention to your present assignment. I've seen this mistake made over and over again: Someone gets excited about what God has promised them but begins to devalue where God has them. And what needs to be understood here is that how you handle your present season comprises the seeds that you will sow into your next season. A friend of mine, Pastor Tyler, says it thus: "To get what God has for you next, we must be faithful in what he has given us last."

God wants you to finish your current assignment strong. God does not want you to look past your current assignment or look down on your current assignment because your next assignment will be great. To be honest, you won't get your next assignment if you don't handle your current one well. People often miss this part of the process. There are lessons in your current obligation that you will need to learn and to master before moving into your next place. Don't allow the temptation of the flesh to move you faster than you should go, forcing you to miss what you're supposed to get in the season that you're in.

The next temptation comprises your feelings. When you're operating in God's process and living in the in-between, it can be very uncomfortable. The temptation is to run from discomfort because we just want to be comfortable and not to have any turmoil. However, I want you to understand that, today, you need to be married to discomfort. In our places of discomfort, we experience the greatest levels of growth. I often think to myself, *Why can't I just learn it from a book? Why can't someone just teach it in a seminar?* But there are lessons that one can only learn by living them. There are things that one can only learn by being tested in the fire of discomfort.

At such times, my feelings can become my enemy. My feelings just want to be comfortable. Warning! Warning! Warning! This is where many of us give birth to Ismael. We feel like we don't want to wait on God because he's taken too long. We step out because of our feelings and quit our jobs and walk away from our only livelihoods. I hear so many people say, "Well, God told me to quit, and God told me to move on. God told me to leave that church. God told me to leave that job."

Then they find that it was their feelings and flesh that got them. We must let patience do its perfect work within us so that we can be mature and complete, missing nothing. We must adopt God's timetable and not our own. When we do that, we can tell our feelings to shut up. The bottom line is that my flesh and feelings are where the Spirit isn't leading me.

The third temptation is fear. The enemy will make you think that delay means denial, that because God hasn't let it come to pass yet, he won't ever let it come to pass. The enemy will tell you you're not good enough, not pretty enough, not smart enough. He will want you to quit simply because he's told you that you don't have the time, the talent, or the treasure to let what God has within you come to pass. It's here that he plays his greatest trick. He knows he can't take the promise from you, so he seeks to get you to lay it down. His goal is to get you to quit, to get you to give up in the in-between because he knows that, if he can get you to give up, he can steal from you what God has for you. He will create the circumstances to try and get you to believe that God will not do what He said He would do.

But God's promises keep you when your circumstances seek to blind you. In these moments, you have to agree with God. Right in the middle of everything going on, right in the middle of your flesh telling you to hurry up, right in the middle of your feelings warning you to just do what's comfortable, right in the middle of your fears trying to tell you that you are not good enough, smart enough, or qualified enough, you must find the faith to say, "I'm moving forward. I refuse to give up. I am more than a conqueror through Christ, who loved me and gave His life for me. I can do all things through Christ who strengthens me." It's here that you agree with God, embrace the season, and continue to move forward. It is here that your faith is developed, your roots are deepened, and you become more mature. This is where patience does its perfect work within you because you are becoming the person God called you to be. You are moving from failure to fulfillment.

God's Timing

Through the years, patience has not been one of my greatest virtues. I often get a vision from God, and then I have to navigate all three enemies seemingly at the same time. My flesh, my feelings, and those fears all seem to come at once, wanting me to move before it's time or to quit before the plan comes to pass. However, I've adopted a Scripture that helps me to navigate the temptations and allows patience to have its perfect work within me. Imperfectly though I do it, I have a standard that I can always come back to because of what God has given me through his word. The Scripture in question is Psalms 31:15. It reads, "*But I am trusting you, O Lord. I said, 'You alone are my God; my times are in your hands...'*" (Psalm 31:15 (TLB)). I discovered this Scripture during one of the more difficult times of my life. I knew God had called me; I understood that God's purpose was going to take time, but I wanted it immediately. This Scripture allows me to rest in God's timing and see that, when God's promise, my prayers, and God's timing come together, there will be breakthrough. It's not that there might be breakthrough. It's not that there could be breakthrough. There will be breakthrough.

The lesson I had to learn was that, no matter where I was or what was going on, if I allowed patience to have its perfect work, if I allowed God to develop me and mature me in the moment, if I embraced the season that I was in and didn't look too hard at the one that I was going to, God's will would come to pass in his timing. I have learned that, in the in-between seasons, God is doing some of his greatest work within me. I have found that my greatest moments of growth have occurred in the times of my greatest discomfort. I have discovered that my faith has grown the most when my fears have been the fiercest. Remember that God's timing is always perfect, His ways are always right, and His plan for you is always good. As you keep those things in the forefront of your mind, you will navigate the in-between season well and get what God has in store for you.

Things to Remember

- *Your ability to be patient will determine how much you accomplish in life.*
- *To get what God has for you next, you must be faithful to what he gave you last.*
- *Remember, God's timing is always perfect, His ways are always right, and His plan for you is always good.*

Chapter 6

Know Your Why

John 18:37b (AMP)

[37]This is why I was born, and for this I have come into the world, to testify to the truth...

When you know your "why," your "what" will have more impact because you're walking towards your purpose. – *Michael Jr. (Comedian)*

A new survey from salary.com reveals that now, more than ever, Americans aren't happy at work. Only 38.5 percent of the 2,000 American workers surveyed said they were "personally fulfilled by the work" they did—a sharp decrease from 59.2 percent in 2012. A whopping 72 percent said they worked primarily for money. When I see stats like this, I am reminded of how many people go through life aimlessly, not really living. So many people never experience true fulfillment because they don't have real reasons for doing what they do. I've seen many leaders cause their teams to lose morale because they are great at telling them what to do but can't give them real motivations for doing what they do.

One of my favorite leadership experts, Simon Sinek, talks about the "Golden Circle." He says it's not enough to know what you do or how to do it. The essence of everyone's motivation is "why" they do the things they do. This is such a powerful statement because when you can connect your WHAT *to* WHY, it changes everything. Understanding your WHY gives you the motivation, the energy, and the perseverance to keep moving when everything around you says, "Stop." When we talk about moving from failure to fulfillment, if you don't have a solid WHY, you'll quit right in the middle of the process.

Whether they are trying to build the fastest computer or the fastest car, every great person who's ever done anything significant has to start with a WHY. The definition of "why" is the cause, reason, or purpose for which you do something. Therefore, the WHY is anything that you do for a specific purpose or a specific reason that fuels your desire. When people don't have a solid WHY, quitting becomes an option, and not finishing becomes inevitable. Your WHY provides the fire in your belly that keeps you moving forward when everything else says, "No." I believe that, when your WHY is off, your life is off too.

The Power of "Why"

Your greatest fulfillment, passion, and prosperity are tied to your WHY. The power of a WHY is most effective when it's tied to something that is near and dear to your heart. When someone's motivation is simply to make more money or to build a better status or make a greater name for themselves, they usually don't have the fire that will help them to persevere when things are difficult. However when they have a solid reason for what they're doing, something that they are passionate about that is connected to their emotions, they have greater resistance to quitting and giving up.

The son who wants to make it in the NFL because he wants to be able to feed his family and spends countless hours practicing and getting better so that he can put himself in a position to take care of them. He won't let injury stop him; he won't let other people stop him; he will push past every obstacle because he wants to make his family's life better. The mother who works several jobs just to make sure she can take care of her family, whose WHY is to make sure that her children have a better life, will work past exhaustion to make sure that she can provide for them.

A solid WHY is one of the most inspiring things you can have to move your life forward in any field. I believe that knowing why God created you and put you on the earth is extremely important. When we talk about being motivated to change or to move forward when you feel like stopping, that's a whole different story. The motivation of some is simply to please God; that of others is to avoid experiencing the pain of the past. Whatever the motivation is, a reason connected to a strong emotion gives you the ability to keep moving forward.

My Motivation

One of my favorite pastimes was going to watch some of the youth from our church playing sports. Most times, they would ask me to come out to a game to support them because their parents wouldn't. It's actually one of the joys of my life to see my kids out there, enjoying themselves playing a sport that they worked so hard to become good at. On this particular day, I was watching one of our students playing football at a local field. As he saw me walking towards the field, I could see the smile on his face through his helmet. He was excited that I was out there to watch him play. I grew up playing sports myself, so I knew the thrill of having someone come out to support you.

A few minutes into the game, I witnessed a child that I didn't know make a mistake on the field. I could tell immediately that the kid was demoralized as he made his way back to the bench. His coach began yelling and screaming at him because of the mistake that he'd made on the field. The coach actually started using cusswords; I guess he wanted to get the child's attention or drive a point home. Sitting on the sidelines, I was mortified that any child would have to endure such a situation. I waited to see if there were parents in the stands that would run to the child's defense or at least confront the coach and let him know that this wasn't the way to handle a youth sport. However, no one came, and the coach seemed to feel his behavior was ok.

I remember walking away after the game, feeling like no child should ever have to endure that type of abuse when playing sports. As a former athlete myself, I was reminded of the tremendous influence that coaches had over the lives of children in their care, teaching them how to play sports. I've often seen sports as a great metaphor for how to live life. If you know how to handle yourself on the field, ice, or court, you'll know how to handle yourself in life. Days went by, and I could not shake that moment at the field, watching the child's face as I listened to the coach berate him. All I could think was that someone needed to do something. Someone needed to create a league where kids could play and learn sports without having to endure that type of behavior from their coach. As those thoughts came rushing into my mind, I could sense the Holy Spirit saying that He wanted me to do it. He wanted me to start the program. At that moment, a burning desire to use the vehicle of athletics to teach kids character in life lessons was born in me. This new passion for sports and the impact that it could have in the lives of youth was birthed in my soul.

Over the next few months, I would make phone calls, set up meetings, and organize opportunities to begin this new venture. It seemed like no one could see what I could and no one was interested in the sports program. I remember wondering over and over again, "Did I really hear from God? Is God really in this?" However, I would get up the next day, and I'd try all over again. I received refusal after refusal after refusal, but, each day, I kept trying. When I look back at that time, I realize that I should have given up early. But there was something motivating me that went beyond every refusal that I received. It was the face of that little boy: the hurt he'd been subjected to by someone that he looked up to. Even though I didn't know him and never saw him again, his face was etched in my soul. I knew I had to do something for all the little boys and girls like him who wanted to play sports but didn't want to endure that. Obstacle after obstacle, challenge after challenge, I kept pressing and kept going until, one day, the door opened. It would be a total of eight years before I saw the dream of my heart fulfilled.

How does a person continue to fight for something even when it feels like they're losing? How does a person continue to go after a dream when it doesn't feel like that dream will ever come to pass? I'll tell you how. When you have a strong enough WHY, everything else takes care of itself. When you have a strong enough WHY, you push past disappointment and overcome every rejection to see your dream come to pass.

My WHY was every child who would ever want to play sports and was looking for a role model, not a dictator. My WHY was every parent who wanted their child to experience life lessons without scars from coaches who were trying to live out their childhood dreams through the kids that they coached. My WHY was so strong that I was willing to do whatever it took to make sure my dream came true. When your WHY is so strong, no mountain is so high, no valley is so deep, and no situation is so horrible that it would stop the fulfillment of your dream. What's your WHY? What problem are you looking to solve? What burden are you seeking to relieve someone of? Spend time with

God, allowing him to bring to the surface a burden in your heart to make someone else's life better. When you see that, you'll find your WHY.

Things to Remember

- *The strength of your* WHY *will push you to win.*
- *Your greatest fulfillment, passion, and prosperity are tied to your* WHY.
- *Whatever the motivation is, that reason connected to a strong emotion gives you the ability to keep moving forward.*

Chapter 7

Do It Afraid

Joshua 1:9 (GNT)

[9] *Remember that I have commanded you to be determined and confident! Do not be afraid or discouraged, for I, the Lord your God, am with you wherever you go.*

Everything you've ever wanted is sitting on the other side of fear. – George Addair

One of my favorite Bible stories is the story of Joshua as he's leading the children of Israel to the Promised Land. Think about this for a moment: You're following Moses, whom God used to defeat an army, part the Red Sea, feed the children of Israel in the wilderness, and get water from a rock. Now Moses exits the scene, and God tells you, Joshua, that you are the next leader of these millions of people. As Joshua, you watch this whole thing play out: from the people's complaints about having to leave Egypt to their complaints about the food in the wilderness and, eventually, their complaints about the Promised Land itself because of the giants in it. Now you have to come after one of Israel's greatest leaders to date. Imagine the fear and anxiety Joshua must feel, knowing that God has given him this incredible task. Even more important, God knows he will be afraid. So He speaks the words of comfort found in Joshua 1:2-9:

> 2 *He said, "My servant Moses is dead. Get ready now, you and all the people of Israel, and cross the Jordan River into the land that I am giving them.* 3 *As I told Moses, I have given you and all my people the entire land that you will be marching over.* 4 *Your borders will reach from the desert in the south to the Lebanon Mountains in the north; from the great Euphrates River in the east, through the Hittite country, to the Mediterranean Sea in the west.* 5 *Joshua, no one will be able to defeat you as long as you live. I will be with you as I was with Moses. I will always be with you; I will never abandon you.*
>
> 6 *Be determined and confident, for you will be the leader of these people as they occupy this land which I promised their ancestors.* 7 *Just be determined, be confident; and make sure that you obey the whole Law that my servant Moses gave you. Do not neglect any part of it and you will succeed wherever you go.* 8 *Be sure that the book of the Law is always read in your worship. Study it day and night, and make sure that you obey everything written in it. Then you will be prosperous and successful.* 9 *Remember that I have commanded you to be determined and confident! Do not be afraid or discouraged, for I, the Lord your God, am with you wherever you go."* (*Joshua* 1:2-9 (GNT))

God speaks these words of comfort and strength to Joshua as he is about to set out for the unknown. However one thing is necessary: No matter what God says, Joshua has to do it. It doesn't matter what God says to Joshua; if he doesn't take this step of faith, he will never get to experience what's on the other side of his fear. So it is with us. We can have the greatest of intentions. We can have the greatest vision for our future, but we have to take a step. One thing is consistent regarding Joshua, you, and me: If we don't act in spite of our fears, we will never get to see our dreams come to life. This is embodied by a phrase that I've learned over the years: "do it afraid."

Understanding Fear

I've heard many people say that fear is only a spirit but the truth of the matter is that fear is a spirit which carries with it many expressions. Whenever we are asked to step into something we've never stepped into before, to go somewhere we've never gone before, or to do something we've never done before, fear is there waiting. Fear is like a thief waiting to steal your greatest desires and dreams from you before you even get a chance to start. One of the major things that happens to us when we experience failure is that we become afraid to try again. We think, "What if I fail this time? What if I mess up this time? What if I jack things up again?" It's like a movie playing in your head, telling you, "Don't do it!" as if it's trying to protect you.

When we allow fear to run our lives, we never do the things we were destined to do. Fear works like this: God tells you to do something, and immediately fear gives you reasons why you can't do it. It says you're not qualified or educated enough or gifted enough to carry this task out. It reminds you of past mistakes and failings that have held you back before. Fear is designed to trap you and keep you locked in a cycle of unbelief. Fear is the opposite of faith. Faith draws to you the very things that you want, while fear draws to you the very things that you don't want. Therefore, if we're going to move forward, we must recognize that fear will be there when we're ready to take a step. When George Addair says, "Everything you want is on the other side of fear," he's giving us an indicator that fear comes to stop us.

There are three aspects of fear we must understand: First, we must understand that fear is a liar. It works in this way: It will always come to you and tell you what you can't do in order to keep you from trying. I call it a liar because the truth is that you are made in God's image and likeness. The truth is that you can do all things through Christ, who strengthens you. The truth is that you are more than a conqueror through Christ, who loves you and died for you. The truth is that, if God asks you to do it, He's already giving you the ability to carry it out with His help. However, the liar, fear, wants you to believe that you are not able to do it. That's why I call him the liar. He always comes to tell you words that God has never said about you.

The second aspect we must understand is that fear carries with it emotions. When you are about to step out into something you've never done before—I call this stepping out of your comfort zone—your enemy, fear, will be there to push you right back into it. Whenever you step out of your comfort zone, he's there to try and push you back in.

Third, he can only be defeated by faith-filled action. This points us to James 1:26, which says, "So *then, as the body without the spirit is dead, also faith without actions is dead.*" To overcome fear, we must respond in faith by acting on the word of God. When we act on what God says in spite of what we feel, we are doing it afraid. Courage is not the absence of fear; it's the ability to act right in the middle of feeling fear.

Stepping Out in Faith

It was a nice summer morning, and I was set for a busy day at work. I remember sitting at my desk, getting my papers ready and preparing for my next phone call. All of a sudden, I felt the presence of God come over me like never before. I couldn't believe this was happening at my desk at work, but it was unmistakable. It was God seeking my attention. I tried to ignore it and get back to work, but I could not. I stepped away from my desk and went to a bathroom stall, where I began to pray.

As I prayed with my eyes closed, God began to show me a vision. It was a vision of three distinct things. The first one was of my son, Daniel, in a suit in a boardroom, conducting a meeting. I didn't completely understand what he was saying, but I sensed in my spirit that God was showing me that he would be successful. The second vision was of my wife. We were standing on a stage together at Oral Roberts University, delivering a message. The third and final vision was centered on a series of buildings with the same name on them. I couldn't make out the name. However, I noticed that there were ten buildings.

I get it. I know this sounds weird. It was weird for me too. But I could distinctly sense that God was calling me to full-time ministry. I remember sharing it with friends and close family and being excited about the prospect of working for God full-time. There was just one problem. No one was offering me a job. Shortly after this experience, I remember sharing with my pastor what had happened and what was in my heart to do in ministry. I didn't know where it would lead. I just knew I needed to obey what the Holy Spirit was telling me to do. Yet nothing came of it. So I continued to pray. I went about my business. Then the day came: My pastor called me to the church and offered me a part-time job running our sports ministry. I was so excited! Here was God doing the very thing that He'd told me He was going to do. A job in ministry: I couldn't wait.

Then came the challenge. To work part-time at the church, I would have to take a demotion at work. I supervised one of the groups in our office, and I couldn't be a supervisor and work this part-time job at the church because of the hours. That was where fear came in. I needed every dollar I could get, and I needed the money from my full-time job. I couldn't take a pay cut even though I was taking the part-time job at the church. It was not going to be enough money to sustain my family. I remember feeling fear in the pit of my stomach for days. I was a door away from achieving my dream, and yet I needed the money from my full-time job to survive. After spending a few days in prayer, I felt peaceful about moving forward and taking a part-time job at the church. I walked into my boss's office regarding my full-time job and told him that I would need to take a demotion so that I could take the job at the church. He was very supportive, but he also reminded me that this would come with a pay cut. With fear in my gut, I said I believed that God would take care of me. I remember waiting for payday to see what would be on my check since I had to take the pay cut. I noticed that it was the same amount that it had always been. I waited another couple of weeks, thinking that maybe they'd gotten the change in late and now I would feel the loss of income. However, my check was the same.

After getting this last check, I went into my boss's office and brought to his attention the fact that they hadn't done anything with my pay. I know this sounds crazy, and many of my friends thought I should have left it alone. But I was turning over a new leaf and wanted to walk in integrity, so I told him. My boss leaned back in his chair and said that the company had decided not to cut my pay because they believed so much in what I was doing. I walked out of his office rejoicing. I learned a valuable lesson through that experience: Fear will speak to you, but God's word never fails. If I had allowed fear to stop me, I would have never experienced the blessing that God had in store for me. By doing it afraid—doing it right in the presence of fear—I saw God open a door that no man could shut.

Things to Remember

- *God is not the author of fear.*
- *Everything you've ever wanted is sitting on the other side of fear.*
- *Faith draws to you the very things that you want, while fear draws to you the very things that you don't want.*

The Power of Humility

1 Peter 5:5-6 (ESV)

5 *Likewise, you who are younger, be subject to the elders. Clothe yourselves, all of you, with humility toward one another, for "God opposes the proud but gives grace to the humble."*
6 *Humble yourselves, therefore, under the mighty hand of God so that at the proper time he may exalt you*

True humility is not thinking less of yourself, it's thinking of yourself less. – C.S. Lewis

Humility is the key to lasting success and continued growth. One of my favorite NFL players is Peyton Manning. He was one of the most prolific quarterbacks to ever play football. He holds many records in the NFL and is known as one of the best quarterbacks to ever play the game. However, you would not know that if you met him. Manning happens to be one of the humblest players you could ever come across. In an interview after a game against the Baltimore Ravens where he threw seven touchdown passes, that was on full display. To fully grasp this accomplishment, you must understand that the Baltimore Ravens we're the reigning Super Bowl champions that year. It occurred on one of the biggest stages of the NFL: the Thursday night season opener.

All eyes were on them and what they might accomplish in the coming season. Yet, in this high-profile game, he torched the Ravens with seven touchdown passes. In an interview after the game, with Frank Schwab asked, "Is this the best game of your career?"

Manning said, "I don't know. I guess I haven't had a whole lot of time to think about it. Our offensive line did a great job protecting against such a tough bunch up front." When asked about his own performance, Peyton pointed to the performance of his team. That was humility. Humility has no desire to take all the credit. Humility has no desire to be out on Front Street, getting all the attention. Humility is the ability to quietly go about your business, gain success, and give others the credit. Peyton Manning is an example of this humility: breaking all types of records and winning Super Bowls but, at the end of the day, consistently giving credit to his team for his success. When a person walks in this type of humility, success continually finds them. The opposite is true for pride. The Bible says that pride comes before a fall. So when we truly understand what humility means, we set ourselves up for greater success and fulfillment.

True Humility

Humility is a term that is often misunderstood. And many people think that humility has to do with a sense of low self-esteem or low estimation of oneself. I've come to know through a powerful quote what true humility is. CS Lewis, author of *The Screwtape Letters*, says, "True humility is not thinking less of yourself; it's thinking of yourself less." This quote is one of the forces that has helped me understand what true humility is. For years, I thought humility was simply thinking less of myself. When someone gave me a compliment, I would say, "Glory to God," or constantly find ways to deflect from what they were saying about me by returning a compliment to them. True humility is the ability to say thank you while giving glory to God. It is not pridefully taking all the glory for myself but recognizing that I played a part in achieving the success. All the glory goes to God, but when a person gives me a compliment, I can also say, "Thank you."

I learned over the course of time that my response was one of my self-defeating responses. I didn't think myself worthy of success because of my mistakes. Hence, I didn't think that I was good enough at anything. I would simply give glory to God with the thought that He almost did it without me. Don't get me wrong. This isn't a shifty way to take credit for what God does in our lives or some weird way of being prideful. If what CS Lewis says is true, humility is my way of thinking of myself less. But he did not say not to think of yourself at all. This was one of the hurdles that I had to overcome over the course of my life with my failures. I had to overcome my thoughts of failure and frustration, replacing them with thoughts that God could do something significant through me. I started this by developing a healthy view of God. Thinking of myself less simply means I don't put all my stock in my ability, my intellect, or my strength; I'm totally dependent on God. Therefore, to me, humility means acknowledging that I am totally dependent on God for my success in every area of my life. Without God, I can do nothing, but, with God, all things are possible. Peter says this type of humility brings exultation from God.

When I focus on my strength and my ability, I may be filled with pride because I am only thinking about me. If I were a failure, I'd be filled with self-loathing because all I would see was what I couldn't do. When I'm filled with humility, I recognize my limitations as a human being without God. At the same time, I recognize my unlimited capability with God. You and I were never created to live within the realm of our own ability. From the beginning, we were created to depend on God. Therefore, my walking in true humility means I'm not focused on my strength or my ability alone but on God's strength through me. So, on my best day, I can say, "Thank you. Glory to God. He did it through me." And, on my worst day, I can say, "Glory to God. I need to let him work through me."

Last Word on Humility

Another facet of humility that is often not talked about is being teachable. One of the greatest aspects of humility is a teachable spirit. When you see this definition or understanding of humility, you really get an illustration of why pride is so dangerous. Pride often says, "I know everything. I don't need any help. I have everything under control." The focus of pride is "I." When a person is filled with pride, they're declaring that they are self-sufficient and they don't need anyone, including God. However, a person with a teachable spirit is willing to learn from anyone. That person recognizes their own limitations and understands their need for others. When a person has a teachable spirit, nothing is impossible to them. Whatever they don't know, they're willing to go after and learn how to do. When a person is teachable, God can constantly develop them and help them grow in any and every circumstance. However, when a person thinks that they know it all and that they have arrived, they cut off the help that's there for them. Peter comments about this:

> [5] *Likewise, you who are younger, be subject to the elders. Clothe yourselves, all of you, with humility toward one another, for "God opposes the proud but gives grace to the humble."*[6] *Humble yourselves, therefore, under the mighty hand of God so that at the proper time he may exalt you.* (1 Peter 5:5-6 (ESV))

Peter says God opposes the proud but gives grace to the humble. The Greek word for grace is *charis*, which refers to bestowing favor. So what we find here is that, when we walk in humility, the favor of God follows us wherever we go. With this favor, doors open that wouldn't normally open. People notice us who wouldn't normally notice us. We experienced the power and presence of God moving in different areas of our lives; we would not have experienced this if we had walked in pride. Remember that the Scripture says that God opposes the proud but gives grace to the humble. So this grace is God's ability and favor, allowing us to do things we couldn't normally do without it. When I walk in humility, I am inviting the presence and power of God to accompany me into every environment that I go into. Talk about being set up for success. That's why humility is so important. That's why having a teachable spirit is so important: You become attractive to those who are around you.

Grace upon Grace

It was a regular Sunday morning, and I was sitting in my normal seat, which was right around the third row. I didn't come into the service with any great expectation or any real desire to experience God on that day. I was simply fulfilling the normal requirement that I attend Sunday morning service as a member of the church staff. I can't say that I was experiencing a weird season of frustration or anything that would warrant my having an intense encounter with God. I was actually in a good place and doing what I loved doing with our sports ministry. I remember sensing the presence of God in a strong way after the first song. I recall hearing the Holy Spirit say, "Get on your knees." I immediately looked around me and saw that no one else was on their knees. We were all standing and worshipping, some raising their hands and some just staring at the worship leader as if they were at a concert.

I could sense the Holy Spirit saying to me, "Get on your knees." It wasn't this audible voice from heaven saying, "Tony, get on your knees." It was an inner knowing that I can't explain: I knew the Holy Spirit wanted me to get on my knees. I remember thinking inwardly—okay, arguing inwardly with the Holy Spirit—saying, "No one else is on their knees. This will be embarrassing. People will think something is wrong with me." Yet, as the first song came to a close, the Holy Spirit wouldn't let it go. I remember the start of the second song and not being able to shake this feeling. At this point, I couldn't even enjoy worship because I was in an inward tug of war with the Holy Spirit.

We normally sang four songs on a Sunday. So I was thinking, "Let me get rid of this feeling so that I can get back to worship." I repented so that I could just get past the feeling and go back to worship. However, the Holy Spirit wouldn't let go of me. By the end of the third song, I finally said yes to getting on my knees. Don't judge me. You've done the same thing many times in your walk with God too. If God asked you to do something that seemed impractical or unthinkable or even embarrassing you would fight too.

When, I finally got on my knees and worshipped, tears flooded my eyes. I remember a deep sense of peace coming over me like a flood. I remember these distinct words that the Holy Spirit said to me in that moment: "Tony, if you stay here in your heart, I will take you to places you never thought you'd go. I will bring you before great men and women. And you will one day be a pastor here at the church." The tears streamed to a greater extent as I continued to worship on my knees. What he was telling me in that moment was that, if I remained humble, teachable, and pliable in his hands, he would give me a life beyond my greatest dreams.

I've never forgotten that moment. Years later, tears still come to my eyes when I recall it: that God would take this broken, often failing man who was deeply flawed and make him such a great promise. At that moment, something shifted within my heart. I begin to live my life with the quest to remain humble. Years later, that promise has been fulfilled in so many different ways, including the opportunities that I have been afforded and the places that I've been blessed to step into. God told me that, if I remained humble, he would do things I'd never imagined. He has actually done exceedingly abundantly more then I even imagined him doing from that day, all because he's given me the spirit of humility.

Things to Remember

- *True humility is not thinking less of yourself; it's thinking of yourself less.*
- *When you walk in humility, success will find you.*
- *Humility means being totally dependent on God for success in every area of my life.*

Chapter 9

Maximize Your Moments

Ephesians 5:15-16 (TLB)

15-16 *So be careful how you act; these are difficult days. Don't be fools; be wise: make the most of every opportunity you have for doing good.*

If you crush it in the now, it will lead to your next. – Sam Collier

I came across a quote a gentleman by the name of Sam Collier. He says, "If you crush it in the now, it will lead to the next." I love that statement because, the way I see it, your now will lead to your next. I see that we are given moments, but we don't always consider them seriously. So we don't maximize them. Many of us think, *My moment is when I get on this stage. My moment is when I get the job that I want. My moment is when everybody's looking. I get enough Facebook likes or enough Instagram followers: That's my moment.* But I want to submit to you today that, whatever moment you're in right now, that's your moment. If you are working a job that you don't like or are in a situation that you're not happy about, guess what? That's your moment, and how you handle it will determine whether the next one shows up.

I run into many people that can't wait to get a new job or a new husband. I'm sorry. We always think the next thing will be better. Well, guess what shows up in the next thing? You. If you're not better, the next thing will be the same as the current one. So ask what God is doing in your now as he prepares you for your next because, if you don't handle your now correctly, your next may never show up. I call this maximizing the moment. Paul tells us in 2 Corinthians 4:17, "*For this light momentary affliction is preparing for us an eternal weight of glory beyond all comparison.*" God is preparing us for a greater weight of glory. So whatever moment you are in is the moment of preparation. Maybe your moment entails going through marriage problems. Maybe your moment entails struggling in school. Maybe your moment entails having a job that you hate. It's a moment, a bleep on the radar, but this little bleep can determine the rest of your life.

Obstacles or Barriers

Paul talks about afflictions. We consider afflictions to be giants. Giants are those things in our lives that we don't like, that we're waiting on God to move us on from. Giants can be sickness. Your giant can be your lack of education. Your giant can be anything and everything that keeps you from moving into what God has in store for you. Giants create big shadows. They stand in the way of something. Your giant is standing in the way of your destiny, your joy, your peace. And what I've learned about giants is this: Your giant's ability to move or not to move is based on how you see.

In Numbers 13, when God told the 12 spies through Moses to go and spy out the land, they did so and said, "God this is exactly the way you said it is, a land flowing with milk and honey." But 10 of the spies said, "Nah, nah, we can't overcome the giants in the land." There were two others who came back: Joshua and Caleb. And they said, "Nah, we are well able to do what God said we could do." What was the difference? They saw the same things, went to the same places, and served the same God, but their perspectives about what they were facing were different. Challenges could either be obstacles or barriers.

An obstacle is something that you have to go around or over, something that hinders progress. A barrier is something that stops progress. When I see my giant as a barrier, it stops me. Some of you view your pasts as your barriers. So you can't get past them. Instead of getting around them, you're stuck, and you say, "I can't get past this." Some of you are facing obstacles, but you've made them seem like barriers and, thus, can't get past your mistakes.

Many of us are facing things right now that we've made so big and large that we think, *I can never get past this. I can never overcome this.*

God said, "If you trust me, I'm going to not only take you around it and over it, but I'm also going to take you through it. The very thing that you thought would stop you is an obstacle that I've allowed to be in place, not so that you can see how great you are, but so that you can know how great I am."

I've found that successful people have the ability to take what unsuccessful people see as barriers and make them simple obstacles to success. You may say, "I tried this. I did that. It didn't work. I tried that idea. It didn't work." Listen, God gave you this idea. God gave you this vision. So what you should do is keep grinding. You should keep seeking because there's a way over this thing. This thing is not the end of you. It's a part of your story. Overcoming this giant will make it easier to overcome the next one. There will be lessons from this fight that you will take into your next fight. That's why it's so important to maximize every moment: Your moments today will prepare you for your moments tomorrow. Each moment is defined by choices. The choices we make today will determine the future we live tomorrow.

When facing your giants, you must make six key choices in order to walk in the victory that God has for you: choose to win, choose faith, choose to believe in you, choose to remember, choose your weapon, and choose your words. If you are going to get unstuck, you must make the right choices. The choices you made yesterday created the reality you live in today. It's time to change your choices.

Choose to Win

One of my favorite Bible stories is that of David and Goliath. David was anointed king but continued to serve as a shepherd. He had to go back to the sheep because God didn't give him the kingdom right away.

God had to prepare him for the kingdom. So there David was with the sheep one day when his father came to him and said, "Hey, your brothers have been away fighting the war. Go take them something to eat."

While taking food to his brothers, David saw the giant Goliath hurling insults at Israel. Goliath was cursing (the Bible actually uses this word) and everybody was afraid because he was a nine-foot-tall giant. They said, "Oh, he's too big."

If you know the history of Israel and the Philistines, you will recognize that Philistine was part of the land of Canaan that God had promised the children of Israel. The Philistines were a resilient group. Israel would fight against them and gain some victory, but not full victory. And so here the children of Israel were again, fighting the Philistine army. What they failed to see was that they weren't fighting the giant in their strength; they were fighting it in God's strength.

Israel was backed by the promises of God but was still afraid of the giant. God is speaking to us right now. He says, "I told you that you would overcome this thing. I promised you that you would come out of this thing. I said, 'We're going to go to the other side.' Why are you so focused on the giant instead of my words? If the giant is in your way, and I tell you that you're going to go to a certain place, guess what? That giant's got to go. But the giant can only go if you agree with me and not with the giant."

So David walked up and said, "Hey, do y'all hear this? He's cursing us. Is anybody going to do anything?"

But nobody did anything. The boy, who had to be 13 or 14 years old, walked up to the King.

He said, "King Saul, let no one lose heart on account of this Philistine. God is going to give us the victory over this giant." Although Saul saw that David was young and inexperienced, he noticed something else in the boy that he couldn't dismiss. There was a confidence in him. David said, "You don't know who I am. Let me inform you: I watch my daddy's sheep. I had a bear and a lion come against me one day, and I was able to take them out. So this uncircumcised Philistine is going down."

Remember the word "uncircumcised." It was significant because it meant that Goliath was not a part of God's covenant. Circumcision was a sign of the covenant. David was saying, "Listen, this dude is not even on God's side. We've got God on our side. We're in a covenant with God Almighty. He can talk and bark all he wants, but he doesn't have Jehovah Jireh with him. He doesn't have Jehovah Nissi. He doesn't have Jehovah Shalom with him. So why are we listening to him? Why are you listening to people that don't even know God?"

I could ask you similar questions: Why are you stuck on what your third-grade teacher said? Why are you stuck on what people said about you on social media? They don't know your God. Why are you letting them define you? God has placed your giant before you, but you've got to make a choice. You've got to make a choice to win.

Choose Faith

I love a statement by Gary Vaynerchuk in his book *Crushing It*. He says, "Being unafraid of making mistakes makes everything easy. For me, not worrying about what people think frees you to do things, and doing things allows you to win or learn from your loss—which means you win either way." Hear me. The first choice you've got to make is this: "I'm no longer going to be afraid to try, I'm no longer going to be afraid to step out." And these steps should be light steps, not foolish ones. It's like taking a step in a direction. I learned this from author Joyce Meyer: You take a step in a direction, see if the peace of God and the hand of God are there, then take another step. When you sense that God is in what you're doing, you take another step. This means you don't just go off and quit your job. That's called foolishness. While you've got a job, take some steps because it's harder to take a step in peace when you don't have a paycheck coming in. So take responsible steps. While you're working, God will begin to show you what direction to go in. When I choose faith, I choose to move forward even in the face of fear.

Choose to Believe in You

Believe in God, who believes in you. When David began to talk to Saul about the fact that he would fight Goliath since no one else would, Saul said, "You're not able to go out against this Philistine and fight. You are only a young man. And he's been a warrior from his youth."

But David said, "Nah, I know what you think, but I know what God showed me about me. Although you're the King, I'm not defined by what you think about me. I'm defined by the Creator who made me. Therefore, I'm going to believe in what God has done inside of me. I'm going to choose to believe in what God has placed in me even if you don't believe in it. What I love about God is this: You don't have to believe in my vision. You don't have to believe in my dream. I have to believe in what God put inside of me. And if you don't believe in it, that's okay. One day you're going to see the hand of God in my life. And you'll be like, 'Oh, that boy knew what he was talking about the whole time.'"

I remember I was working at a company and God was dealing with me on the subject of being in full-time ministry. I began speaking to some of my friends and telling them that God was calling me to full-time ministry. You know what? People hear that all the time. I hear it all the time. I said, "No, no, no, no, no. God's called me to full-time ministry now."

The people who didn't know Jesus said, "Man, that's crazy." But the thing that got me was that the people who did know Jesus didn't believe it either.

"I get all of that wisdom and everything. But he's calling me to full-time ministry." When God opened the door for me to get my first job in ministry, people said that was crazy. I said, "Just watch." When they said that didn't make any sense, I said, "Just watch God." Now, 16 years later, I'm still working in full-time ministry. The very thing that they thought was crazy about and said I couldn't do, God did for me. If I had listened to all the voices around me, I would never have done what God told me to, and I would still be doing the very thing that I hated doing daily. That's why you've got to choose to believe in you.

Choose to Remember

When you're in a fight for your destiny, health, or family, you've got to choose to remember. You have to remember the last time God delivered you, the last time you felt like this, the last time you thought there was no way out. You've got to remember the last thing that God did for you. That's why it's important to journal when you're walking through difficult seasons. Journaling allows you to chronicle what you're experiencing so that you will have something to remember it by.

I remember looking at a journal that I had years ago. And I remember reading a bit that said, "God, I don't know how you're going to fix this. I don't know how I'm going to come out of this." Now, I look at that journal, and I laugh. Not only did I come through 10 years ago, but I've also got journal after journal chronicling how I came through challenges again and again over the past 10 years.

You've got to choose to remember. When David was facing the giant, Goliath, he said, "Wait a minute. I remember that I faced the lion and I faced the bear and God delivered me. The same God that delivered me there is the same God that's with me now. And he's going to put this uncircumcised Philistine into my hands." Just like David did, you've got to remember who has your back.

Choose Your Weapon

David was getting ready to go out and fight Goliath, but King Saul wanted him to use his armor. So Saul outfitted David in the King's armor: a bronze helmet to protect this head, a coat of mail to protect the chest. Afterward, David strapped on Saul's sword and then discovered that he could not move because he was not used to the restrictions of the weighty armor. David said, "I'm not used to these things. How can I attack an enemy when I can't even walk?" So he removed every bit of Saul's armor and chose to fight just like he'd fought the lion and the bear.

Everybody thinks that you should undertake a task the way they did it. And if you don't do it like they did it, they say you're doing it wrong. They tell you that you have to go this way or that way, you have to go to this school or company, or you've got to handle it this way. Your response should be "Listen, that may be the way that you got through, but that's not the way He's taking me there. So I'm going to choose my weapon. And my weapon is me: my authenticity, my personality, my gifts, and my abilities.

God is offering a million ways out of your situation. Let me say this again: God is offering a million ways out of your situation. When somebody says you've got to be a certain way to get what God has for you, stop. Principles transfer, but you don't need to be that person. You can learn from their principles, but you don't have to fight the way they fight. When you choose your weapon, comparison dies. When you choose to be you, to lead the way God has called you, you are no longer comparing yourself to your neighbor. You're not in this to see who can do it the best. You know why? Because they can't do it like you. They weren't created the way you were. They don't have your "this." They don't have your "that."

When mentoring others, most people try to turn them into mini-mes. God didn't ask anybody to take on someone else's image. He said, "You are created in my image and my likeness." So, while somebody's mentoring you, you should make sure they're not trying to turn you into them. My goal when I mentor you is to make you the best version of yourself. You are enough. You are enough. And when you find out who you really are, you will succeed without breaking a sweat. You are a designer's original. Nobody has been created like you, talks like you, thinks like you, or is like you. When you fall in love with you, you are untouchable, and nobody can compete with you or compare to you. As a matter of fact, every time you try to compare yourself to somebody else, you demean who God is because you're saying, "God, you made a mistake with me." However, God says you are enough because I say you are enough. Your authenticity is your weapon.

Choose Your Words

One true statement I have heard over the years is that whether you say you can or you can't, you're right. That's because whatever comes out of your mouth is the fruit that you will eat over the course of your life. You may say, "I'm not smart enough. Yeah. I don't have their mix of gifts. I'm not as talented as them." But listen: every single one of us has enough talent to do what we were created to do. Every single one of us has enough gifts and ability to do the very things that God breathed life into us for. So when you stop looking at other people and letting them define your life, you will be more fulfilled. Choose to say about yourself what the Father says about you. You are fearfully and wonderfully made. That's what God says about you.

David said to the Philistine who was talking to him, "You come against me with a sword and a spear and a javelin, but I come against you in the name of the Lord."

And you may say to those who seek to hurt you, "You come against me with this puny little rumor; this puny little bit of gossip; this puny little thought about what I've done in the past. You come against me with my lack of education or my lack of 'this' or my lack of 'that.' You can say, "I am who God says I am. God is fighting on my behalf."

God will catapult you over those with master's degree and the PhDs. When you choose to speak God's word over your situation, He can take you from stuck to unstuck. From failure to flourishing. Your words have power and, when you use them in conjunction with God's word, you will experience God's help.

Things to Remember

- *If you crush it in the now, it will lead to your next.*
- *Your moments today prepare you for your opportunities tomorrow.*
- *The choices we make today determine the future we will live tomorrow.*

Chapter 10

Walk Away from the Old

Philippians 3:13-14 (AMP)

[13] Brothers and sisters, I do not consider that I have made it my own yet; but one thing I do: forgetting what lies behind and reaching forward to what lies ahead, [14] I press on toward the goal to win the [heavenly] prize of the upward call of God in Christ Jesus.

God, grant me ***the serenity*** *to accept the things I cannot change, courage to change the things I can, and wisdom to know the difference. – Unknown*

On any given Sunday, men and women all across our nation sit with remote controls in their hands, watching their favorite football teams play. With the creation of NFL Network, we now have the ability to change the channel to watch whatever game we want. Many times, there are breaks in games or we get bored; so we flip the channel to another game. The beauty of NFL Network is that we have so many choices of games to watch that we never have to get stuck watching games that we don't enjoy. The remote is the mechanism by which we turn off one game and turn on another. This incredible power in our hands gives us the opportunity to go back and forth to watch the games that we truly enjoy.

So it is with our minds. When we truly understand the power that we have to choose, we no longer have to watch channels that don't benefit us. Many of us are stuck watching channels of defeat, channels of hurt, or channels of failure when all we really have to do is change the channel to one that makes us feel better. We have the ability not to focus on negative thinking or thoughts of defeat; we can actually focus on thoughts of victory and success. The greatest challenge for many is knowing that they hold the remote to change the channel in their minds. Before you are ever defeated in real life, you will be defeated in your mind. And before you are ever successful in real life, you'll have to be successful in your mind. When we understand this truth, by the power of God, we gain the ability within us to walk away from the thoughts that hold us captive to our past failures and mistakes.

The prayer "God grant me the serenity to accept the things I cannot change, the courage to change the things I can, and the wisdom to know the difference," has been prayed all around the world in churches, homes, and recovery groups. The whole idea is to ask God to help people change the things that they can change and to know what they can't change. I often use the word "control" in the place of "change." However the premise is the same: "May God help me to know what I can and can't change or control."

One of the things that I've learned is that I can control and change how certain things affect my life. I've learned over the course of time that I'm empowered to overcome my past and others' opinions, and to face forward for the dreams in my heart and to experience fulfillment in ways I never thought that I could. As I have continued to grow and develop, I have learned that my responsibility for my growth is greater than I thought it was. I have often spent time waiting for God to change me or to help me in particular areas of my life. But I've discovered that God will never do for me what I can do for myself.

One of the areas that I had to take responsibility for was how my past and other people's opinions of my past impacted my life. I would often use this as an excuse for my lack of success. I would say to God, "No one's ever going to listen to me. No one's ever going to believe in me because of the mistakes that I've made." That would be my excuse for not going after more. However, one day God showed me that he had given me the power to overcome every mistake and every bad decision but I had to do the work.

In his writings to the Philippian church, Paul gave us the principles that would allow us to begin making our way forward and that would no longer allow the past and others to hold us back. He wrote the following to the church:

> [13] *Brothers and sisters, I do not consider that I have made it my own yet; but one thing I do: forgetting what lies behind and reaching forward to what lies ahead,* [14] *I press on toward the goal to win the [heavenly] prize of the upward call of*

God in Christ Jesus. (*Philippians* 3:13-14 (AMP))

From his writings, I understood that the mistakes from my past did not have to define the heights I would rise to in the future. Paul, who had persecuted the Church and placed Christians in jail, was no longer bound by his past. In one portion of the Scripture, he referred to himself as the worst of all sinners. Yet he wrote most of the New Testament. I often wondered how he could make so many mistakes and do so much wrong and yet turn his life around to do so much good. Think about the churches that he started and the people who were saved under his ministry. So many people would experience life changes by virtue of his writings. Yet he was the worst of all sinners.

In that Scripture in Philippians, he gives us a picture of how he was able to overcome his past to be who God had called him to be. He speaks of forgetting what lies behind. This thought alone is life-altering. He had the ability to take all of his mistakes and all of his failures and put them behind him. I believe you can't look backward and forward at the same time. In this Scripture, Paul teaches us how not to look backward. He says, "Forget it." How simple a thought, yet how difficult a walk . For us to leave our failures behind and move into a place of fulfillment, we must first put the past behind us. As Paul states, "Forget it."

One of my favorite scriptures in the Bible is found in Isaiah. It says, "I, *yes I, am the One and Only who completely erases your sins, never to be seen again, I will not remember them again. Freely I do this because of who I am.*" (*Isaiah* 43:25 (TPT))

God says, "I will not remember your sins again." So, when my sins came rushing back into my mind and feelings of guilt and shame started to overwhelm me, I had to remember it wasn't God. He promised that, when I repented of my sins, he would forget them and never remember them again. So how could he bring up what he didn't remember? If God could forgive my sins, then so could I.

Paul says, "*Reaching for what lies ahead, I pressed towards a mark.*" He says, "*I leave the past behind then forget it,*" but he also says, "*I'm pressing forward towards the mark.*" We now see how he was able to have such an incredible impact moving forward after all the mistakes that he made. He not only forgot the past, but he also focused on the future. What worked for Paul can work for us. As we forget about the past and focus on the future, we find the fulfillment that God has had for us the whole time.

During this process of growth and development in my Christian walk, I learned three key principles that helped me to navigate the waters of change. These three principles would be the guiding force behind my building new memories. I believe that, if you follow these three principles, you will build the life that God intends for you right in the midst of others not believing in you:

- *Stop seeing yourself in your past;*
- *Stop seeing yourself in others' opinions;*
- *Start seeing yourself from God's perspective.*

Stop Seeing Yourself in Your Past

One of the key factors of being able to move on from the past is not seeing yourself in the past. As long as you see yourself as the person who made all those mistakes, you will continue to gravitate towards them. If, however, you move forward, stop seeing yourself in your past, and start seeing yourself in the future that God has in store for you, you gravitate towards that future. This doesn't mean you should deny the reality of the choices that you've made. It simply means that you should learn from them and keep moving. I love this quote by an unknown author:

> *Today is the tomorrow you thought about yesterday! Wherever you are today, you made an appointment to be there yesterday! Your estimation of what you deserve has manifested. Don't complain or cry about it, change it! Expect more! When you change your mind, you change your life. Nothing has to remain the same!*

This reminds me of the fact that the reality I'm living in today is based on the choices I made yesterday, so if I want a different reality tomorrow, I simply need to make different choices today. Your today is the sum total of the choices you made based on the information you had. When you have new information, you make better choices. All we have is today. Today, make choices according to who God says you are. Today, know you are the righteousness of God in Christ. Today, know you are not a loser or a reject. You are God's masterpiece. Today, you are successful, beautiful, strong, and powerful due to the power at work within. Now, get up and act like it. If you messed up, get up. If you blew it, get up. Press on, press on, press on.

Stop Seeing Yourself in Others' Opinions

The second thing I had to do as I moved forward was to stop seeing myself in others' opinions. I struggled with allowing myself to be defined how other people saw me. With this came the desire to please everyone around me. I had to recognize that the way people saw me was based on the decisions that I'd made in the past and the mistakes that they'd seen me make. At times, it felt like I would always live under the shadow of my mistakes because it seemed as if others did not want to release me from them. But, one day, I found a Scripture that set me free:

> [25] *The fear of human opinion disables; trusting in GOD protects you from that. (Proverbs 29:25 (MSG))*

I realized, that, as long as I lived in fear of other people's opinions, I was not trusting God. That lack of trust would place me in a constant cycle of trying to please those around me and not being able to fully walk in my God-given destiny. I understood a long time ago that, when God gave me a vision or spoke a word to me, He produced the faith in me to fulfill that vision. I believe it, so I know God can bring it to pass. The challenge was that I always wanted others to see it. I always wanted them to cosign on what God had given me. If they didn't, I would question whether God had really spoken in it. However through the above Scripture, I learned that, when I trusted God I didn't need to lean on other people's opinions.

Therefore, you are no longer bound by the opinions of others. You're free to be who God has called you to be. And, no matter what your past, no matter what you've done wrong, what God says about you matters most. God has already made his mind up about you. God is narrowminded when it comes to you. No matter what people say about you, no matter how badly you mess up, God still says you are His masterpiece. No matter how ugly you act, God still says you are His masterpiece. You must learn to stop needing everybody to agree with what God says about you and simply agree with God. Be free from the opinions of man today.

Start Seeing Yourself from God's Perspective

Finally, after I stopped seeing myself in my past and stopped seeing myself in other people's opinions, I could start seeing myself from God's perspective. You have to see yourself from God's perspective. When you do that, the other two perspectives fade. I live by John 15:15-16, the Scripture below:

> [15] *I do not call you servants any longer, for the servant does not know what his master is doing; but I have called you [My] friends, because I have revealed to you everything that I have heard from My Father.* [16] *You have not chosen Me, but I have chosen you and I have appointed and placed and purposefully planted you, so that you would go and bear fruit and keep on bearing, and that your fruit will remain and be lasting, so that whatever you ask of the Father in My name [as My representative] He may give to you.* (John 15:16 (AMP))

When I first read that, I about jumped out of my skin. Knowing that God chose me, that he appointed me and placed me purposefully was one of the greatest revelations of my life. Then, no matter how bad things were, no matter what other people thought, I could say with confidence that God had chosen me. He says, "I have ordained, appointed, commissioned, and anointed you for what I want to, and no other opinion matters. If you believe in me over what your past says, believe in me over what your friends and family say, I have a destiny in store for you that no man can touch. I am the one who called you.

"I am the one who anointed you. I am the one who set you apart. If you trust me on the journey, I will take you to a place you never thought you would go. You will stand before people you never thought you would stand before. When you truly understand that you are chosen by God, I will bless you in ways you didn't even think to ask for. You are chosen, called, anointed, and appointed by God to do great works and great exploits."

You are not what others have said about you. You are not the mistakes of your past. You are a divine idea in the mind of God. You are God's masterpiece, created for his use. You are empowered to prosper. You are not defined by your past but by the future that God has in store for you. Today, walk into the future by walking away from your past. It's time to build a new tomorrow.

Things to Remember

- *Before you ever become successful in real life, you'll have to be successful in your mind.*
- *What God says about you is what matters most.*
- *Walk into the future by walking away from your past.*

Chapter 11

Reframe Your Mind

Romans 12:2 (AMPC)

[2] Do not be conformed to this world (this age), [fashioned after and adapted to its external, superficial customs], but be transformed (changed) by the [entire] renewal of your mind [by its new ideals and its new attitude], so that you may prove [for yourselves] what is the good and acceptable and perfect will of God, even the thing which is good and acceptable and perfect [in His sight for you].

Change your mind, your life will follow. – Karen Casey

I have been framed

We've all been framed. By the time we were five or six years old, we were given versions of ourselves by those who were raising us. Whether you grew up in a two-parent home with siblings or you were parented by a single mom, you were given a framework of your life early on based on what you were taught, what you saw, and what you experienced. This framework was used to develop your subconscious. Subconscious thoughts are the seed of your memories and your well-formed beliefs about yourself, your world, and your capabilities. In these formidable years, we develop limitations regarding who we are and what we're capable of doing. In a healthy environment, we learn that nothing is impossible to us. If we set our minds to it, there is nothing we can't achieve.

We have an unlimited source of ability and potential, and a high ceiling over our lives. However, for most of our lives, this was not the environment that we grew up in. Many of us grew up in dysfunctional situations that left us feeling incapable of doing anything significant. Imagine with me if you will: Remember when you were a child and you wanted to be a doctor, a lawyer, a policeman, or even a fireman. You had the outfit; you wore the uniform; you played doctor; you were a policeman. Feeding your imagination at such a young age allowed you to be anything and everything that you wanted to be. Yet, as you grew older and the limitations of those around you begin to seep in, you no longer saw what you dreamed of as attainable. That's what framing does. It places you in a box of self-imposed limitations that seems almost impossible to get out of.

This framing helps us make assessments of what we can and can't do, where we can and can't go what we can and can't achieve. An equation I like to use helps give a picture of how this framing works:

Environment + Experience + Education = Esteem

Through this equation, we can see how framing begins at an early age. Let me explain.

1. *Environment - My environment is characterized by where I lived, the surroundings of the place where I lived, and the people that I lived around. It includes my parents, my neighborhood, and my socioeconomic status. It's simply the environment that I grew up in that influences my thoughts of myself.*

2. *Experience - My experience is characterized by what I saw growing up, that is, what I saw in my parents, what I experienced at school, what my teachers told me, what my friend said about me, the trauma I may have experienced as a child, a divorce my parents may have gone through. All of these experiences helped create the framework within which I live as I get older.*

3. *Education - My education is characterized by how well I did in school, the school system that I grew up in, the level of my education (formal and informal). The level of my learning determines the frame that I live in.*

When you put my environment, my experience, and my education together, they begin to form my esteem or what others call self-esteem. *Self-esteem is one's confidence in one's own worth, abilities, or self-respect.* Through this, we see that, when someone's framing is off, their self-esteem is off. Then they can't truly assess their abilities, capabilities, or achievable accomplishments. Poor self-esteem happens when my environment, my experiences, and my education don't line up with the dreams in my heart. I'm left feeling inadequate, unqualified, and unable to do anything that I dream of doing because of those factors. Therefore, if I'm going to be the person whom God has called me to be, I must change the frame.

Reframing

In this next section, I want to help you reframe your thinking from the negative defeating thoughts to the thoughts of the person whom God really created you to be. I'm not a therapist, but these key factors helped me overcome the negative thinking of my past to tap into the unlimited potential that God has placed inside me.

The goal of reframing is to take those negative thoughts that were developed in you by your environment, your experience, and your education and turn them into thoughts that help you achieve your highest goals and your greatest form of fulfillment. There are a couple of different things that you must do to begin the process of reframing. First, you must be aware of where your negative thought traps lie. You have to become aware of when and where your negative thoughts surface. In so many words, you have to start considering what you think about. You can no longer allow random thoughts to go through your mind unchecked. You must pay attention to all of the thoughts that go through your mind so that you can check the ones that are defeating you.

Second, you must question the thoughts that come into your mind. Ask, "Is this accurate? Is this thought helping me or is it hindering me? What can I gain by accepting this thought? Does this thought move me forward or does it hold me back?" When you begin to question the thoughts that come into your mind, you have the ability to reframe them.

Third, you must interrupt the narrative. Now that you're aware and ask questions, you must begin to interrupt the thoughts that come into your mind. It's important to take those negative thoughts and turn them into positive thoughts. The Apostle Paul said the following:

> [2] *Do not be conformed to this world (this age), [fashioned after and adapted to its external, superficial customs], but be transformed (changed) by the [entire] renewal of your mind [by its new ideals and its new attitude], so that you may prove [for yourselves] what is the good and acceptable and perfect will of God, even the thing which is good and acceptable and perfect [in His sight for you]. (Romans 12:2 (AMPC))*

Paul writes that, to be transformed, you must have an entire renewal of your mind with new ideals and new attitudes. It is this renewing of the mind that reframes how you see yourself, your abilities, and even your past mistakes. When, by learning who he is, I allow the Word of God to reframe my environment, my experience, and my education, I am in the process of reframing my life. When I take my thoughts through the filter "Is this what God says about me? Does this line up with what the word of God says about me?" I begin reframing those old negative thoughts and experiences that have held me back and hindered me from moving forward. I now reframe them in such a way that God can launch me forward and move me into my destiny.

It doesn't matter how many mistakes you've made, how many times you've blown it, what neighborhood you grew up in, what experiences (traumatic or not) you've had, or what level of education you've had to this point, when you begin to allow God's thoughts to overcome yours, you have the ability to be who God called you to be. When you reframe your thoughts, you reframe your life. You are more than the environment you grew up in. You are more than the experiences that you've had. You are more than your education says you are right now. But this only works when you believe and you put in the work to reframe your thinking. It doesn't happen by accident; it only happens with intentionality. You determine how much of God's will you can experience in this life when you allow him to transform your thinking into His thinking.

Reframing My Thoughts, Reframing My Life

Years ago, while sitting in a one-bedroom apartment, I remember thinking, "How did I get here?" The walls were dirty. There was a stale smell throughout the apartment. The kitchen was horrible, and the bathroom was deplorable. Yet there I was. That was what my life had come to. My own decisions had led me to that place. I'd had a pretty good life, but I hadn't been able to keep from sabotaging it. I'd made some decisions over the prior couple of years that had led me from owning my own home to living in a dirty one-bedroom apartment. I'd had so much going for me at the time, or so I'd thought. I'd lived with nagging thoughts: "You don't deserve this life. When people find out who you really are, they will not like you. Who do you think you are?" I'd been brought up in a toxic environment that had caused me to grow up with low self-esteem. Even when good happened to me, I just didn't think that I deserved it, and so I would somehow sabotage it.

As a child, I went through traumatic experiences with my mom's bipolar disorder. I tried so hard to keep her healthy that I didn't know that I was making myself unhealthy. The experiences that I had as a young child, I wouldn't wish on my worst enemy. I didn't get to choose where I grew up or my experiences. The negative impact trickled into the classroom, and I went from being an A student to getting all Fs in my first semester in high school. It was a perfect storm. My environment was toxic, my experiences were traumatic, and my education was poor. And there I sat, alone, hopeless, and even wanting to commit suicide. I felt like such a failure and I just knew there was no way for me to come out of it. Then I had an encounter with God.

One day, I was in my apartment all by myself, experiencing one of my lowest moments. My thoughts confirmed every bad thing that had happened to me and every bad decision that I'd made to that point. I found myself sitting there in agreement with every negative thought from my past: "You're not good enough. You're not smart enough. This is what you deserve. This is the life that you deserve to live." Then God came into the room. This may sound crazy to you, but I could sense him. It was as if He were a real person standing right in front of me. I remember saying to Him, "You can have my life. I surrender. I have proven what I can do with this life that I have. Today, I fully surrender it to you. I want what you want for me for the rest of my life. If there is any good that you can bring out of this life, I give it to you."

At that moment, the presence of God filled my apartment and my heart, and I made the choice that I would no longer allow my environment, my experience, or my education to be excuses for how I lived my life. I would no longer allow what I'd gone through to define where I was going. So I set out on a quest to reframe my thinking. I began listening to sermons, reading the word of God daily, becoming aware of my negative thoughts, and questioning whether they were helping me or hurting me. I began to attack those thoughts with God's word. And the repetition and consistent daily engagement started to change the way I thought. When my thinking changed, my life did too. I began to see the light at the end of the tunnel, and my life's experiences started to line up with this new education that I'd received in God's word.

This whole process started with my choice to no longer be defined by my environment, my experiences, or my education. I learned a couple of valuable lessons. The first one was that I couldn't change the environment I grew up in and I couldn't change the trauma that I'd experienced but I could change how I saw it. There were no longer things to look back at and use as excuses for having a less than great life. They were now flashes of God's grace that brought me through and help me to survive. Second, I could control my education. I could control what I knew and the information I took in. Armed with this new truth, I moved forward in life, allowing God to teach me and train me in his ways so that I could live out the life that he'd called me to.

Things to Remember

- *Your belief system (your frame) was developed during your childhood.*
- *When you reframe your thoughts, you reframe your life.*

Chapter 12

It All Works Together

Romans 8:28 (TLB)

[28] *And we know that all that happens to us is working for our good if we love God and are fitting into his plans.*

The messes of life can create the most beautiful things. – Ebony Rayford

I am what you call a foodie. I love great food, but I must say I'm pretty particular about the food that I eat. On many of my missionary journeys to different places around the world, one of my greatest challenges was eating foods whose origins I didn't know. One of my good friends, who was born and raised in Louisiana, made a great jambalaya. One day, I made the mistake of asking what he put in his jambalaya. Once he described the ingredients, I was immediately put off by the thought of even trying it. He put things like sausage, shrimp, canola oil, and all these different spices in. It just didn't seem like they would taste good together.

After some effort on his part to convince me, I decided to try his jambalaya and see what it actually tasted like. I was blown away, and my taste buds were set ablaze. I couldn't believe this whole mixture of foods could taste this good. None of the things he described had seemed to go together, but, in the end, the incredible mix of herbs and spices tasted fantastic. That's how it is with life sometimes. We often think that the good times are the only things to be celebrated, and we are all too eager to forget our mistakes, our failures, and the bad seasons. However, God takes everything in our lives and mixes it together to make a beautiful symphony of what he calls our purpose. The good, the bad, and the ugly in God's hands make one of the most beautiful things you could ever imagine.

In Romans 8:28, the Apostle Paul says, "*And we know that all that happens to us is working for our good if we love God and are fitting into his plans.*" This Scripture reminds me that all things, no matter how good or bad, work for me and fit in his plan because I love him. All things include my mistakes, missteps, failures, and sins. When I began to see life this way, I would no longer allow guilt and shame to dominate my life because I'd learned that nothing that happened in my life had caught God off guard. He'd already seen it, made a way for it, and had seen me through it. Therefore, I could get up and allow him to keep directing my path.

One of the enemy's greatest tricks is to make us believe that the things that we've done wrong make what God wants to do in our lives impossible. I submit to you today that God prepared you for your failures as He was preparing you for your future. He knew full well what you would do when you did it and He still didn't change his mind about you. As a matter of fact, according to the Scripture cited in the previous paragraph, He makes it all fit into his plans because we love Him and are called according to His purpose. Therefore, we must get up and continue to go after what God has called us to do in spite of ourselves. Just like the jambalaya has different types of ingredients to make it taste wonderful, your life brings different ingredients together to make a beautiful picture. A dash of success, a smidgen of failure, a pinch of sin, and a cup of victory all make up the life that God has called you to live, enabling you to accomplish his purpose for you.

Let God Redirect You

One day, I was driving down a local highway, trying to find my way to a store I'd never been to before. Although I'm highly familiar with the streets in the city in which I live, I love using the GPS because it allows me to know how long it's going to take to get to my destination. I know this makes no sense if I know where I'm going, but I don't like to waste time, so I use my GPS.

As I was driving down the highway, I missed my off ramp and had to go up a little farther. Then I noticed that the GPS begin to redirect me. Missing my off ramp added another 10 minutes to my journey. The one thing that stuck out to me as I was traveling was that the GPS didn't start to direct me from my original location. It started from where I was. Starting over would have added another 30 minutes to my drive, but since the GPS picked up where I left off, it just added another 10 minutes. By allowing the GPS to redirect me, I eventually made it to my destination, but I got there a little later than I wanted to.

That's what I love about God. At times, God is like my GPS. He gives me directions to get to a destination according to his timing. However, there are times when I choose to go in a direction that he did not want me to or to do something that he didn't want me to. He doesn't say that he will no longer give me directions to the place. He doesn't say I can no longer go. He simply waits on me to acknowledge that I made a mistake or repent and then we pick up where I left off. Today, God is not telling you that you have to start from the beginning. He is telling you that you have to admit to your mistake. When you repent of your sins, you are simply saying, "God, I'm sorry for going in the wrong direction. I'm sorry for not following your guidance in this particular area of my life." And when you do that, God will redirect you and get you back onto the road to your destiny. It may take you longer than it should have, but you'll still get there.

I've learned that we all make mistakes. We all sin. We all do things that displease God; none of us is perfect. When we make mistakes, we are consumed with guilt. We think we've disqualified ourselves from receiving blessings and that our mistakes are bigger than our God. Well, we think that our mistakes are bigger than God's ability to forgive us. That divorce, that abortion, that lie, that situation that haunts you: You think that it's so heinous and so big that God can never forgive you. We all have something in our lives that we believe we can put into that slot that says, "No, you're not worthy to be blessed by God. You're not worthy to fulfill God's plan and purpose for your life." But I've learned over the course of time that I am not the author of my own destiny. I didn't write my own script. I didn't create myself. And I didn't create the purpose in my life. God did.

You didn't create me either. Your family didn't create you. As for the people in your life that may be saying you're not worthy, you're not worth it, or you're not qualified, guess what? They're not your creator. Since you didn't create yourself and they didn't create you, none of you are qualified to say what you can or can't do. Your destiny is not in the hands of a punitive God who is looking to beat you down at every corner. Your destiny and purpose are in the hands of a loving God that wants you to win more than you want to win.

When I wrapped my mind around that thought, I could look at it and say to God, "You knew what you were getting when you called me. You knew what you were getting when you saved me. You knew what was wrong with me. You knew my idiosyncrasies. You knew what I had walked through. When I was a child, you knew. You knew. You knew. It was not a surprise to you."

But you say, "Tony, you don't understand what I've done. You don't understand where I've been. You don't understand who I've hurt."

Yeah, I don't. He does. And He's still calling you by name. He's still calling you out of darkness and into

His marvelous life. He still sent His son to die for you. The Bible says that, in spite of our sins, He sent his son to die for us. Jesus died on the cross so that, no matter what direction we were going in, if it opposed what God wanted, He could redirect us. He could provide the pathway back to God's grace, God's love, and God's purpose for our lives. It's time to let God redirect you.

Years ago, I went on a mission trip to Mexico with a group of middle school students. It was my first time to venture outside the United States, and I was extremely excited. This trip couldn't have come at a better time. I'd just emerged from three years of walking away from the everything and giving up on my calling. At this time, God was beginning to restore my sense of purpose and destiny. I didn't expect to do much beyond babysitting the middle school students. However, I couldn't have been more wrong. God had something significant in store for me. I remember waking up in Mexico, basking in the sunrise and thinking about God's goodness. I had no idea what they had in store for me.

New to this experience, I knew we were there to minister to the less fortunate in the city of Acuna. After breakfast, to my surprise, one of the leaders walked over to me and asked me to preach the message at a nearby village. I was blown away. It had been a while since I'd really preached a message, but, even more exciting, I'd never preached a message away from American soil. With nervous excitement I prepared to preach on Sunday.

As was our custom, we would gather at the beginning of each day and pray, asking God to help us reach the citizens in the city of Acuna. At this time, the leader of the trip began to prophesy over different people in the prayer circle. My eyes were closed. I was just enjoying the presence of God. I heard her call my name. She walked towards me and began to lay her hands on my head and pray. The next words that came out of her mouth would change my life forever. She said, "Tony, the Lord is showing me several doors in front of you. However, he wants you to choose only one door." She said that this door was the smallest of all the doors, and I would have to let go of something to enter.

At that moment, I knew exactly what the Lord was asking for. I knew that He was telling me to walk away from something that was still tying me to my past. I remember feeling like a weight had been lifted off my shoulders because I knew that if I walked away from what God was asking, I would walk into a new level of freedom. At that moment, all of the guilt and the shame for the previous few years were washed away, and I started to feel brand new. I thought that, by simply walking away and repenting of my past I would become totally free. However, it wasn't until I let go of the mental entanglement that I experienced the freedom that God really wanted me to have. Then, I sensed God redirecting my life and setting me back on course to fulfill his purpose and plan.

Things to Remember

- *God takes all things in our lives and mixes them together to make a beautiful symphony of what he calls our purpose.*
- *God prepared for your failures as he was preparing for your future.*
- *God makes all things work together for your good.*

Nothing Wasted

John 6:12 (EHV)

[12] When the people were full, he told his disciples, "Gather the pieces that are left over so that nothing is wasted."

Nothing goes to waste on the journey of life. Both good and bad experiences shape your mind and heart for what is to come. – Leon Brown

While doing some background research on the New Testament, I stumbled across this incredible truth. I love studying the Bible, and understanding the culture and background behind it, which makes it come to life. One of the often-unknown facts about the Apostle Paul is that he wrote several of his books while sitting in prison. Philippians, Ephesians, Colossians, and Philemon were all written while Paul was sitting in a jail cell. I'm not talking about a jail cell like the present-day ones but a dark and damp one, oftentimes unbearable to live in.

While imprisoned, he found the strength to write and encourage the other churches. He had no idea that the writings that took place at such a difficult time and in such a difficult season of his life would become the backbone of the Church of the future. He had no idea that, in one of the darkest moments of his existence, his writings would bring life to so many millions after him. He had no idea that, as he persevered through his challenges, his works would help others do the same.

I believe Paul understood as he wrote that there was nothing in all Creation that could separate him from God: not jail, persecution, betrayal, or heartache. Therefore, he could look at this most challenging moment knowing that God was with him and understand that it was leading to a greater purpose. He could understand that although those years were often called the silent years but not the wasted years. Even though he was in this unthinkable situation, he knew that, to God, nothing was wasted. Knowing nothing is wasted encourages us to recognize that God does something with our pain, our heartaches, our difficulties, and even our mistakes. God doesn't waste anything. He uses every bit of it—the good, the bad, and the ugly—to bring about his plan in our lives.

Not Linear

I run into many people who think that fulfilling God's purpose is a linear line. The story goes, "I give my life to Christ, I find God's will for my life, and I live happily ever after." But what most of us don't understand is that God's plan for our lives is filled with many ups and downs, many peaks and valleys. Some values are created by life circumstances, other people's decisions, and what would seem to be other people's random acts of stupidity. However, when you read the Bible, when you see the lives of those in the Scriptures, you understand that it is not always a straight line. As a matter of fact, none of the heroes of faith experienced a straight line. As great as Moses was, he was a murderer. As awesome as Abraham was, he was a liar. As incredible as David was, he was an adulterer. Each one of these men is listed in Hebrews 11 as a hero of faith. That tells me that this walk is not linear but comes with ups and downs, some of our making.

I believe that God is not looking for a perfect performance but for a perfect heart: someone who seeks after righteousness and sometimes misses the mark but continues to get up. When I understand this, I can truly see that, no matter how bad my mistakes have been, God is not through with me. I find great hope in the fact that the Bible was not written about perfect men and women who lived perfect lives, fulfilling God's perfect will. It is filled with people, humans who, though they tried to do right with all their hearts, sometimes failed miserably. That's why I believe we must all embrace the process. The Father knew what He was getting when He got you, and He is not surprised when you blow it. This being our understanding, we must embrace our mistakes and learn from them so that we can become better. When we do that, nothing is wasted.

God is Waiting on You

Now that you know that nothing is wasted. You can see that every single moment, every mistake, and every bad decision can be used by God. What are you going to do? You have been sitting on the sidelines for too long. You have been waiting to feel like you are forgiven and cleansed of your past mistakes. I have come to tell you that God has already forgiven you and cleansed you and is now waiting on you to take your place. When Jesus died on the cross, he paid the price for every wrong thing that you'd ever done. Since he's paid the price for it, why do you keep paying the price by wallowing in guilt and shame. Jesus's work at the cross was complete. You can never pay him back for what he did for you. So why are you waiting to get up once you feel like you've done enough good to earn your way back? You are back already.

God has already made a way for you and everybody who has ever failed to get back up again, but he won't do it for you. He is waiting on you to get up and take your place. He is waiting on you to get up and go after your calling again. He is waiting on you to get up and follow that dream again. Stop waiting on your feelings to give you permission to get back up again. It's now time to walk by faith. According to 1 John 1:9, "*If we confess our sins, he is faithful and just to forgive us our sins and to cleanse us from all unrighteousness.*" So it's time. It's time to dust yourself off . Shake off the grave clothes and come forth like he told Lazarus to. It's time to pick that pen back up again and start writing that book. It's time to enroll in those classes and start going after your degree again. It's time to dust off that business plan, get your LLC and start moving towards that business. It's time. It's time. It's time. You are the one holding this up, not God. It's time to step into your future and move from failure to fulfillment.

Notes

Maxwell, J. C. (2018). *The Maxwell leadership Bible*. Thomas Nelson.

Isaiah 43:25 TPT - - Bible Gateway. (n.d.). https://www.biblegateway.com/

www.ingramcontent.com/pod-product-compliance
Lightning Source LLC
Chambersburg PA
CBHW071352090426
42738CB00012B/3094

* 9 7 8 1 9 4 3 3 4 3 3 0 0 *